Lucy-Anne Holmes is a writer and founder of the successful 'No More Page 3' campaign. Her last novel, *Just a Girl, Standing in Front of a Boy*, won the Romantic Novelists' Association's 'Rom Com of the Year' in 2015. She lives in Hertfordshire with her partner and young son.

Also by the Author

Fiction
Just a Girl, Standing in Front of a Boy
Unlike a Virgin
The (Im)perfect Girlfriend
50 Ways to Find a Lover

Non-fiction
How to Start a Revolution

Don't Hold My Head Down

LUCY-ANNE HOLMES

unbound

First published in 2019
This paperback edition first published in 2020

Unbound
6th Floor Mutual House, 70 Conduit Street, London W1S 2GF

www.unbound.com

Text design by PDQ

A CIP record for this book is available from the British Library

ISBN 978-1-78352-877-6 (trade pbk)
ISBN 978-1-78352-621-5 (trade hbk)
ISBN 978-1-78352-623-9 (ebook)
ISBN 978-1-78352-622-2 (limited edition)

Printed and bound in Great Britain by Clays Ltd, Elcograf S.p.A.

1 3 5 7 9 8 6 4 2

If sexual pleasure were divided into ten parts, only one part would go to the man, and nine parts to the woman.

As told by Tiresias in Ancient Greek mythology

If you don't follow your bliss, how will you find it?

Beth Stephens

The way you make love is the way God will be with you.

Rumi

When I stand in front of another and I love myself entirely, when I love my face and my thighs and my breasts and can ignore all the bullshit that people trying to sell me stuff tell me.

When I love the woman that I am.

When I take the stories of all those who have gone before me, and all those who are here now, who suffer because they are women, those who are raped, murdered, beaten, cut, denied a voice, a vote, an education, when I take their stories and hold them to my own, when I draw on the strength of the women who fought for my rights to vote, to earn, to own property, to be able to have sex for pleasure.

When I stand in front of another knowing that my body is miraculous and that I am wonderful. I am love. I am truth. I am strength. I am woman. I am mother, daughter, sister, ally, healer, visionary, mystic. I am fucking magic.

When I look into the eyes of another and I accept their love and their respect and their wonder.

And I say,

'Come, touch my breast, gently with your fingertips.'

Well, when we do that, I think the earth moves a bit, and the tide turns a touch quicker.

CONTENTS

At some point I should really start this book.

THE SEX BOOK

Hello, I'm Lucy, the writer of this sex book you have in your hands. I've been referring to it as 'the sex book' as I've been writing it, and in the long periods when I haven't been writing it, it's been lolloping around on the sofa in my mind, feet up, not going anywhere. I've been calling it the sex book because there's rather a lot of sex in it. It might even have been called *The Sex Book*, had someone else not already pinched that title. However, it will very soon become apparent that I am no sexpert.

The writer Beverly Cleary said: 'If you don't see the book you want on the shelf, write it.' This book is my attempt at doing that.

You see, glossy pictures of different sexual positions, and advice such as 'tell him what you like' weren't cutting it for me. I'd been having sex for years and years, yet I still felt like a novice. I longed for a book, or a mentor, something, anything, to help me navigate my sexuality. But the book I needed also had to know that I felt a little bit broken in this area, that something fundamental was missing for me. I didn't want it to assume I was a strong, powerful, sexually confident woman, because I felt galaxies away from being so. No, this book needed to know that when it came to sex and relationships in general, I still felt like a girl.

I never found the book I was looking for, but I did go on a journey and find some gold. Now, I'd like to share the treasure.

Disappointing wank

All great stories start with an inciting incident, an experience that catapults the hero onto a journey of discovery they will never forget. Mine starts with me having a wank to internet porn.

It's not quite Dorothy and Toto running away from home in *The Wizard of Oz*, is it?

I'll set the scene. It was half past nine at night. I'd drunk two pints of strong European lager and a 'cheeky half' in a pub beforehand and was now sitting fully clothed on an unmade bed trying to find something on the internet that turned me on.

This wasn't a particularly unusual situation for me. I'd been using/watching/waiting for porn to buffer for years. 'If you're feeling horny then you turn to porn' was something I'd learned not from my mother or the convent school I went to, but from the culture I lived in. There's loads of people having sex on the internet for your viewing pleasure, I had been told, in subtle and not-so-subtle ways. Joey and Chandler from *Friends* watched it. Samantha from *Sex and the City* watched it. Alan Partridge watched it. Everyone was at it. Porn was mainstream, everyday. I'd never really questioned it, or thought about it, it was just what it was.

Looking back, although I'd used it, I wasn't exactly a fan of it. Mainly because one thing that my internet porn fiddles had always done was . . . no, not facilitate an orgasm. One thing that my internet fiddles had pretty much always done was make me feel horrible afterwards. Yes, it was weird, but every time I masturbated to porn I'd always feel a little bit ashamed, a little bit sad, a little bit 'urgh, I don't really like myself now' after. I remember discussing this with a bloke who used porn a lot.

'How do you feel afterwards?'

'Oh, yeah, really terrible and worthless,' he'd replied.

My behaviour post-internet wank supported this. I didn't throw open my window like Julie Andrews in *The Sound of Music* and sing, 'I've just had a wank to porn', I didn't post a Facebook status update informing my friends and family, I didn't tweet, 'Just had a wank to porn! ☺ #wanking'. I deleted my computer's history, I washed my hands and I lied to my mother about what I'd been doing if she called.

Finding something that I liked on these sites could be pretty laborious. What tends to arouse me is people, and especially women, really enjoying themselves. People I sense are acting pleasure doesn't do it for me, neither does 'straight to penetration' sex, or 'fourteen-minute blowjob prior to penetration' sex. So it would generally take me a while to find something that aroused me. It's like normal shopping, where you see lots of bits you definitely don't want before you find that which you like. In the world of online porn that means you see a lot of stuff.

That night I saw an image of a girl – and I say girl, because she looked like a girl, a beautiful blonde teenager – with a man's penis squirting semen into her face. This is not unfamiliar in online porn. It wasn't the act that jolted me – I was used to that – it was how young the girl looked. I found myself wincing at the screen, hoping she was OK.

I cleared my computer's history and I sat there cogitating. I thought about the girl. And then I thought about myself. Now, you might well be sighing at me, 'Whoa there, the woman's bound to be fine, she just looked young. You had a disappointing wank, no need to write a book about it.' But it got me thinking, and as I sat there mulling all this over, I was typing bits and pieces into Google. 'Good sex', 'great sex'. Everything led me back to the same free sites, these garish cornucopias.

The epiphany

Now, I didn't have children at the time, but I had four nieces, amazing young women, and I thought about my youngest niece, curious about her sexual awakening, doing the same Google searches I was doing, getting the same porn sites over and over, and it made me feel a bit sad. This was the sex we were giving our young women and men, and there didn't seem to be any clear alternative, or at least, if there was, it wasn't very easy to find. When I thought about my nieces, these young women I loved, I wished somehow that the sex being presented to them was different.

But what was the sort of sex I wanted for them? I wasn't sure, but I wanted it to be more respectful. I didn't want them to have to pretend to enjoy getting semen in their faces if they didn't like it, or to be forced to gag on a penis if they didn't want to, or to think that the be-all and end-all of sex was penetration. I hoped there would be tenderness in it. And I wanted them to be able to shape the sex they had for themselves, for it to be more mutual, and more, well, beautiful. There didn't seem to be much beauty in what I was seeing.

I typed in the words 'beautiful sex'. The search results included a thirteen-minute video of a lady in lap-dancer shoes giving a man a blowjob while he held her head down. There was also a small clip of a film called *Kama Sutra* that played while an advert flashed up with a teenager in a low-cut top and the tagline 'Shag a slapper', and an article entitled 'How to make beautiful women have sex with you'. Oh, and one website offering pornographic clips with titles like 'Daddy loves to hatefuck daughter. Jap cute schoolgirl gives facial cumshot blowjob to geek on'.

Wow, I thought, if someone had said, 'Here you go, human race, here's this thing, it's called sex, it's an amazing, loving union between two people, where you celebrate and pleasure each other, and it ends in waves of bliss. Take it, human race, and, just for a laugh, see just how far you can debase it,' I'm not sure we could have done a better job than we have.

Charities,[1] teachers,[2] the prime minister,[3] everyone, it seemed at the time, was worried about the impact porn was having on kids. We'd heard that it is where they're getting their sex education from. 'Daddy loves to hatefuck daughter. Jap cute schoolgirl gives facial cumshot blowjob to geek on'. Hmmm. I could see why people were giving it some thought.

But then I considered myself. I was hardly making sex glorious in my own life. There I was at thirty-five, cleaning my computer's history after wanking to internet porn. And when I really thought about it, I realised that I was thirty-five and I hadn't even skimmed the surface of how amazing sex could be. That was rather a sad realisation to have. I'd been sexually active for over twenty years, but, during those twenty years, I hadn't really been that proactive about it. I wasn't thinking about what I wanted and how I wanted it. I hate to say it, but sex was something that sort of just happened to me. I was willing, more than willing, keen even – but I was always an actor in, rather than a director or writer of, the show.

My friend has a saying: 'If you always do what you've always done, you'll always get what you've always got.' I was realising that I didn't want to get what I'd always got in the realm of sex. And what I really wanted was nothing like the sex I found online. I didn't want some sort of painful endurance test, I wanted something slower, more gentle, more creative, more beautiful. I wanted to get good at it, to learn how and where to touch a man, and where and how I liked to be touched, and I wanted to feel safe and respected. And maybe, just maybe, if I explored this for myself and wrote about it, then one day a young woman curious about sex might type the words 'beautiful sex' into a search engine and not be terrified by what she found.

So I decided that instead of merely going along with it, I would finally, after thirty-five years, start stepping into my sexuality and shaping it. Blimey, it felt powerful, like an epiphany, and I'd always fancied having one of those.

Although there was one small problem: I had no idea how I was going to go about it.

The sorry story so far

You may well be wondering what I'd been up to for the last thirty-five years, if it had only just dawned on me that I could start shaping my sexual experiences in the way I wanted. So here is a timeline of the defining moments of my sex story pre-epiphanic wank. It's a sorry story, I'm afraid, but I'm sharing this plotless web of randomly accumulated experiences as I think it offers a bit of insight into why, as a grown woman, I felt so lost in the world of sex. When I speak to other women their stories are always different, but similarly arbitrary, confusing and very often sad.

Age six: I would play with myself with twigs behind the curtains in the living room

One early memory I have is of standing behind the curtains in the family living room playing with myself. I did this a fair few times. I'd gather small twigs from the garden and touch the area in between my legs with them. I've always been a nature lover. I was obviously aware that it wasn't the social norm to be playing with this part of my body, hence me hiding behind a curtain, although I hadn't quite cottoned on to the fact that everyone outside could see what I was getting up to.

Age seven: Played Page 3 girls

I had one friend and when I went to her house we would pretend to be Page 3 girls in her bedroom. One of us would stand topless on her bed posing and pretending to be a Page 3 model, the other would make admiring comments about the other's breasts which we'd heard men use when they looked at Page 3.

Age eight: Caught playing with another girl's bare bottom
This incident is burned on my brain with shame. I was with a friend and we were disturbed by an adult. My friend was lying down on her tummy with her knickers down. I can't remember what we were doing or what game or role play we were in, but I do remember the adult walking in and the feeling of mortification that hit me. Afterwards I tried to avoid the adult, and was told that my knickers were worn to keep my bottom warm. I don't know what the adult would, could or should have said or what I'd say now to a little girl in the same situation. But I was properly embarrassed about this for years.

Age nine: Reading the sexy bits in *The Thorn Birds*
A dog-eared copy did the rounds in my school playground.

Age nine: Teacher took us to the big girls' toilets and showed us the sanitary-disposal unit
This doesn't really have anything to do with my development as a sexually empowered woman, except it was the closest I remember getting to sex education.

Age nine: Feeling aroused
I was staying the night at a childminder's house with my younger niece. It was late. I was alone in a small living room watching the television. I think the childminder was upstairs tending to my niece, who was having trouble sleeping. There was dancing was on the telly. It's funny, as I was writing this I was trying to remember the style of dancing and what sort of programme it

could have been. Hot Gossip, the Arlene Phillips dance troupe of the eighties, came into my head, so I Googled it and I think I found the exact show on YouTube that I was watching that night. I want to describe Hot Gossip as 'a sexy dance troupe' for people who don't know about them, but I'm afraid if I use the word 'sexy' you'll assume it's just women in few clothes dancing provocatively. This was the eighties, though, and sexy and flamboyant was territory for the men as well. In this programme, the men and the women were given equal sexy billing. They were pretty much wearing the same thing in most dances; in one they all wear pants and vesty tops, in another both men and women wear stockings and suspenders. And there is something raw and energetic about it that stirs you up a bit sexually. What I am trying to say is that this isn't the fully clothed bloke stood there with lots of women in high-cut swimsuits writhing around him 'sexily', or the fully grown woman dressed as a girl, all wide-eyed and pouting that we might think of today.

Anyway, according to the YouTube clip, I had my first orgasm three minutes and two seconds into the programme. It was when a male dancer in gold-satin Tarzan pants and cowboy boots ballet leaped across the stage and then did three pelvic thrusts into the camera. It was the pelvic thrusts that did it. I found myself gyrating in my seat, arching my back a little and pressing my thighs together, and feeling something I had never felt before. Afterwards, I thought the childminder would know that there was something different about me, and I would get in trouble, or she would tell my mum.

Age ten: The AIDS leaflet

Everyone was talking about this leaflet with gravestones on the front of it that arrived through the door. I remember reading it and seeing words like 'contraception'. I would then confidently say things like 'you need contraption' without having any idea

THE SEX BOOK | 9

what I was on about. It was about the time I was dancing around singing 'Like a Virgin' and similarly not having a clue.

Age ten: Watching sexy telly was always a bit challenging
Watching anything sexy on the telly with others would always make me uncomfortable. My body and breathing would respond to the sex on the screen and I would worry whether people around me could tell.

Age thirteen: An instructional manual that came with a teen magazine, which told me how to give a handjob, complete with diagrams
I hid it under the rug in my bedroom and looked at it a lot.

Age thirteen: Praying to kiss a boy
I went to a convent school. I was itching to get cracking with boys, hence I implored God to help me out on this one.

Age thirteen: First time I witnessed a male orgasm
I remember a boy and I tussling fully clothed when I was thirteen or so and him suddenly ejaculating in his jeans and going home. I also remember his sense of shame and embarrassment, and neither of us mentioned it afterwards.

Age thirteen: I asked a boy on a ferry crossing to a French exchange trip to French kiss me as I was going to be fourteen in two days
He did.

Age fourteen: First time being aroused with a boy
The first time I remember really being aroused by a boy was at a friend's parents' house. They were at work or away, and we had the lounge to ourselves. We lay on the sofa, kissing and groping.

His hand went inside my bra and really slowly and gently he played with my nipples. It was the first time I realised how sensitive my nipples were. I remember feeling wave upon wave of arousal through my whole body. I wasn't thinking, 'Oh, this will lead to sex.' I wasn't wanting more to happen, I was just really coming adrift at those sensations.

Age fourteen: My first handjob
Despite the illustrated instructions in the magazine supplement, my first handjob was pretty appalling and didn't end in his orgasm. You know that sign you do to indicate things are really good, where the tip of your thumb and the tip of your forefinger touch to form a circle? Well, I did that and went slowly up and down his shaft. For ages.

Throughout my early teens: Did you do this/that?
I remember the sexual aspect of being a teen characterised by a sense of ticking things off a list. 'Has he fingered you?' 'Have you have had sex?'

Age fourteen: Lost my virginity
I was fourteen when I lost my virginity. My diary entry from the time says, 'I know this is right, I love him.' I had been going out with him for five weeks. Juliet had already killed herself over love by that time in her life, so perhaps I shouldn't sit here in my thirties and knock the strength of feeling of my adolescent self.

The event itself was neither sensual or erotic. It happened on a friend's bathroom floor and I spent the whole time asking if the condom had split. 'But I haven't come yet,' the bewildered young chap would say each time I made him remove his penis and check.

While I really liked kissing boys, I don't think I lost my virginity at fourteen because I was keen to explore sensations of arousal that were new to me. I wanted to have sex in the same way I wanted to smoke cigarettes and marijuana or drink alcohol: I thought these things would make me interesting, cool, grown up and therefore desirable.

Age fifteen: First time watching porn
I first encountered porn via a German VHS tape (yes, back in those days). We were teenagers and a male friend's parents were away or at work and we all bundled round and watched it. I didn't really know what to do. I felt aroused but didn't know whether I was supposed to say that or not. I wasn't really sure how you were supposed to watch porn. I spent the whole time paranoid the change in my breathing was going to give me away.

Age eighteen: Masturbation
I had been having sex for four years before I worked out how to masturbate myself to an orgasm. It took a fair bit of work. I was living with a female friend at the time and she had been able to orgasm for years. I went into the bathroom one day, intent on practising, and called out to her for advice and instructions as and when I needed them.

Age nineteen: Porn magazines
I was alone one day while a boyfriend was out and I found his porn mags. (They tended to be under the bed or down the back of the radiator.) I was anxious to find out about this world of sex that men seemed to have access to. The first time I read one, I became very aroused and had an orgasm while reading one particular story. The story was about a woman who had a boyfriend. She was dressed up one night in a long skirt, breasts spilling out of her top, no pants, stockings. I can't really remember all the details of the story, mainly because I used it as

a fantasy for masturbation for years, so the details changed with my imagination. I think when she was out in a club two men were pleasuring her in a subtle way. The story was all about her pleasure, I know that. And I would always look for other stories that would arouse me, but they never seemed to be quite so much about a woman's pleasure, and I always felt a little disappointed after that.

Age nineteen: Porn films

I found his porn films too. I would quickly watch them when no one was around and have furtive orgasms by pressing my hand subtly against my clothed self. It was always just a clitoral orgasm; I had no idea there were any other kinds.

The videos I watched then were nowhere near as 'hardcore' (porn-site language) as things I've seen since on the internet. But the basic roles that each gender played were the same. The men were always the seekers of sex, and the ones in control. The women were young. They tended to always be appraised first by the man – 'let me see your tits', 'look at those tits', 'show me your pussy/ass', etc. – and then he (or he and a friend) would wop out an erect penis and she would get on her knees and so on. The woman would enjoy it, or seem to, most of the time, but would never say what *she* wanted. Sex was always something that was done to her, or that she was led to do.

Age twenty-two: Sexually assaulted after a party

I was asleep and I woke up and a man was touching me intimately and masturbating over me. I left the flat quickly. It was the middle of the night and I walked through London, feeling ashamed, asking myself what I had done wrong. I told a friend who told me she'd been raped in the past; she'd told hardly anyone about it. I sat inside with the curtains drawn for a few days afterwards.

After that
I careered through my teens and twenties having more and more sex, always feeling that there was something in this sex business, but never really knowing what. I really liked kissing and I'd feel arousal and pleasure when my breasts and nipples were caressed, but with penetration, well, it was more uncomfortable than anything. Still, I did it, generally fuelled by drink and drugs, hoping that somehow I was going to get what all the fuss was about. I only ever had quick clitoral orgasms, and never the really great orgasms that I know I am capable of now. As I got older and porn became more available, I started having sex that involved more positions. Quite often it would hurt.

And there we have it, the sorry story so far. Sex, it was something I did but had never mastered. I sensed that I had been vaguely in the right area for a long time, and yet nowhere near where I actually wanted to be, a bit like driving round and round the M25 but never getting to London.

Still, it was going to be different from now on. I was on a mission. A sex mission. Check me out!

The Fuckit List

If you always do what you've always done, you always get what you've always got. I knew I wanted something different in the realm of sex – but what was it I actually wanted? Old-school pen and paper in front of me, I sat and thought about the question for a good while. I asked myself honestly what I would like to experience, and it struck me as odd that I hadn't done this before. I was always writing 'to do's and wish lists in other areas of my life, trying to sort out the tangled ball of hopes and dreams in my mind and turn them into something tangible and physical. But not when it came to sex. And yet when I did turn a bit of focus into this area, I found I wrote effortlessly, and lots.

Although I find myself feeling a little embarrassed about sharing my answers to this question with you now, which is a bit odd, considering you're already acquainted with my masturbatory habits.

OK . . . here goes.

1. Slower sex
Sorry about this one if you were you expecting something a bit more ball gag and latex to start with. But it struck me that what I really wanted was sex that went at a slower pace. I wanted to have time to work out what was going on, what I liked, how I liked it, and what he liked or didn't. I felt that for so long sex had been swept up in speedy routines, and I wanted to break it down to basics, take it apart so I could put it back together. I wanted to take time to build up sexual energy and see where it took me.

2. I'd read that women were capable of fourteen different types of orgasm. I wanted to have them!
I really wanted to get acquainted with my own pleasure.

3. I wanted to ejaculate
Women can ejaculate; online porn calls it 'squirting'. And from the online clips I've seen of it, it really is a sort of ongoing jet spring that fires out of a woman's vagina. It looked pretty badass in terms of a physical release and I wanted to experience it.

4. An all-over body orgasm
Oh, go on then!

5. I wanted to properly learn how to pleasure a man
What I wanted, nay, needed, was some nice uninterrupted time

with a man and his penis. Basically, I wanted to feel confident with a penis. Because it struck me that like a lot of things, for me this was a lot about confidence. Some people can look in the fridge and find a bit of old cheese, some yogurt and a stick of celery and make dinner, because they are confident cooks. I'd look in the fridge, see those things, Google the ingredients, traipse through pages of recipes before giving up and having toast – I don't have a clue. Mind you, there is far more help available to someone should they want to improve their confidence in the area of cooking than there is if someone is feeling similarly scholarly about handjobs. Anyway, there you have it: I had a handjob phobia and I wanted some penis practice. I quite liked the idea of holding a man's pleasure in my hands, perhaps inviting him to visit, saying, 'Knock on my door at eight p.m., be clean and prepared to get naked, and don't plan anything for after.'

6. I wanted to explore sex with a woman

Was/am I a bit gay? Weeeell, yes, definitely, probably, maybe. Gah, it's all a bit confusing. In my head and in my porn tastes I'm definitely bisexual, but in my real life, except for a few *incredibly* drunk situations in my twenties, I'm straight. I did want to explore sexual intimacy with women but was very aware that it's not that easy a thing to make happen. Asking my close girlfriends if they fancy getting jiggy with me didn't feel like the way to go, and I couldn't ask strangers, and if I approached my gay friends I feared their reaction would be 'get away, annoying curious straight woman'. I felt a bit in the dark, and worried I'd go about it all the wrong way.

The list was shortish and therefore doable. You know how it is: if the to-do list is too big, it overwhelms and doesn't get done. It just sits there on the pad, mocking and addling you.

'Well, that should be enough to be getting on with,' I thought breezily, enjoying the high that follows the writing of a succinct list. This sexual odyssey-ing is easy.

SLOW SEX – A BUMPY START

The slow-sex prologue

It was slower than slow. For a long time we didn't even touch. We twisted and hovered around each other. A strange contemporary dance piece: 'Two Sunburned People on a Sofa Touching Each Other with Their Breath'.

My bosom Mills-and-Boon heaved. Oh crikey, did I want him to touch my bosom. Have I always loved the word 'bosom' this much? Although I feared that it would be it for me when he actually did touch my bosom. I might let out a moan that could rouse the dead, or at the very least the chap who was asleep upstairs; I was liable to orgasm while still firmly clothed and before we'd even kissed. Oh my goodness, did I want to kiss him! I had never wanted sex with someone so much. I was arousal soup. And sloshing about with all this sensory anticipation was awesome in itself. Turned on? I was turned UP TO THE MAX, BABY.

Gently he explored my body. Yes, my whole body – if you know me, you might want to sit down for this – even my feet. Bits of me became the most surprising power points of arousal. His fingertips brushed the back of my knee. I groaned. 'Calm down, Luce, it's your knee,' my inner critic said, but I ignored it as he was slowly working his way up my thigh. Oh wow, we took our time. That first nip on my nipple and there I was convulsing in space. We looked into each other's eyes, I felt connected to him through the whole experience. I sensed his delight in me, and in the sex, and his respect for me and for the act that we were doing together.

It was slow sex, and it was fucking beautiful. Beautiful fucking. Now, you'd assume that I'd jump up afterwards and start singing 'ai, ai, yippee', wouldn't you? Well, I didn't. I cried. I lay there naked and I wept. I am so not cool.

'Why are you crying?' he asked.

'I didn't think I deserved to be touched like that,' I said.

He kissed me, and that phrase *I didn't think I deserved to be touched like that* kept repeating in my mind.

How exactly do you get a sexual odyssey off the ground? Anyone?

My journey to me finding slower sex was reeeeeally, reeeeally, I'm sorry to say this, slow. I didn't just grab a fella and say, 'Shall we have us some of that slow sex stuff?' Nope, my journey to slower sex was so long that I have even given the pursuit of slow sex its own prologue to assure you of my success for those times when you'll be wanting to give up on me entirely. The journey to being able to ask for what I wanted clearly and without shame or embarrassment, and then experience what I wanted without shame or embarrassment, went on and on and bloomin' on in a bumpy and bonkers but ultimately quite brilliant way.

In my defence, it's one thing to valiantly sit there with a cup of Yorkshire Tea and an éclair writing a sex wish list. It's quite another thing to get out there and negotiate and do these things with REAL PEOPLE. I didn't really have a clue where to start with all this reshaping my sexuality malarkey. I was a repressed English convent girl, for goodness' sake. But there was one thing

SLOW SEX – A BUMPY START | 19

that had been mentioned to me by a friend, and with no other options I thought I might as well have a go at it.

A single girlfriend had told me how she had been propositioned by a chap she knew. He was a nice bloke, and handsome too. He was a massage therapist, and he'd suggested that they get together one night and, if she felt comfortable, they might try some tantra together. Tantra! I'd heard of that! It was that hippy sex thing Sting did that people took the piss out of. Sting was supposed to have seven-hour bonking sessions. Although seven hours was a tad longer than I'd had in mind, with absolutely nothing else to grasp on to at this point, tantra seemed like it might be what I was looking for. I found myself curious and excited by the fact that tantra seemed to be offering an alternative to the normal way of doing sex as a single person. Normal sex for me took place when so drunk that I had barely any recollection of what happened, save for the occasional flashback that made me put my head in my hands and whisper, 'Oh my God,' the following day.

An article I read online told me that there are tantric exercises that you can do together. When you do them, 'Potent orgasmic energies reportedly move through you . . . Tantra is said to offer sexual and spiritual ecstacy . . .'[1] Potent orgasmic energies, sexual ecstacy, now we're talking.

The chap had told my friend that exploring this didn't mean they were in a relationship, that there was no pressure, so she could continue pursuing other people if she wanted, but if she was open to doing this with him, then great. Their friendship was important, so they'd discuss everything beforehand. There'd be none of the usual awkwardness the next day. No *now what? Should I call? Will he text? What was his name again?*

It was an original way of doing things. I was inspired. Very. This could be the sexual revolution I was seeking. I bought *The Complete Idiot's Guide to Tantric Sex.*

I read it and I quite liked the sound of tantric sex. It was all about touch, breathing, eye contact, taking your time, respecting each other. I was definitely down for trying a bit of it. The language wasn't for everyone; for example, he had to ask you if he could enter your 'sacred space'. Now, in principle, I liked this, it was definitely better than some of the things I'd heard in porn (and in real life, for that matter). But I am British, and therefore practically hardwired to hear those kind of words and guffaw.

Still, on the whole, I was motivated. I bought another book on tantric sex. I felt like a sexual pioneer, willing and able. There was only one slight problem, and it was something I should probably have addressed earlier: I needed a bloke.

This part was tricky. It's not every fella you can say, 'Hello, you look nice, would you like to learn tantric sex with me?' to. You wouldn't ask Wayne Rooney, for example. In fact, nothing against them, but most footballers were out.

Tantra was all about breath, looking in the eyes and touch, so I was on the lookout for someone with hands and eyes, who breathed. Then I had a bit of a genius idea: I would tell men about my friend's tantra proposition in order to gauge their reactions. If any seemed interested then maybe they could be contenders, and I would ask them if they wanted to have a go with me.

For a good while, the search didn't go well. Every single man I told the story to snorted and said, 'Excellent way to get a girl in bed, that is.'

But then I meet this chap. He was English, he seemed sensitive, he was tactile, he had lovely blue eyes, was proficient at breathing and he listened intently without scoffing when I told him my story. It was him!

I decided I was going to ask this lovely sensitive man if he would like to learn tantric sex with me. Yes, because I was a confident and assertive woman finding a new way of navigating my sexuality.

Me asking this fella if he wanted to do tantric sex with me

A bus stop. Near a chip van. Midnight.

I'm wearing my running shoes, my black baggy mid-calf-length trousers that my sister says I should never wear out in public, a floral cagoule and a woolly hat.

Him, sitting on a bench. Me, standing, hopping nervously from one foot to the other.

Me: Um, er, er, um, I um, gosh, I'm, er, oo, gosh, sorry, I'm really embarrassed, er, I wanted to ask you something, um, er, golly, um . . . *(Suddenly hot in the cheeks and clammy underarm)* C-c-c-c-could I ask you something? Um, er, should I ask you something? Do you think?

Him: *(Starting to look quite frightened)* Um, I don't know. Should you?

Me: Well, you, er, you know I mentioned that my erm . . . *(I suddenly start speaking very, very quickly)* you heard me talking about how someone asked a friend of mine if they wanted to meet up and do some tantra?

Him: *(Eyes like a fox about to be run over, nods)*

Me: Er, well, oh my God . . . I'm soooooo embarrassed. *(Touching my cheeks)* Whoa, really very hot now . . . er, er, would that be something you might like to do? With meee. Ahhhhhhhhh *(The sound of a very very quiet scream),* I have to go. Bye. Gaaaaaahhhhhh.

And so I ran away – the running shoes were very useful – saying 'ohmygodohmygodohmygod' repeatedly in a very high register.

Obviously, I couldn't look him in the eyes or talk to him ever again.

Five days passed and I brilliantly managed to avoid talking

to him or catching his eye, a bit of a feat considering we were working together. Eventually, though, it became impossible to completely ignore the fact that he existed. One night a group of us, including him, were out. I was at the bar, buying a round of drinks, he was standing next to me. I couldn't look at him, but I did manage to say, 'Would you like a drink?' to which he responded, 'Thank you, I'd love an orange.' I then ordered the round of drinks and forgot his orange juice.

> Me: *(Looking at the floor)* Bugger. Sorry I forgot your orange juice.
> Him: Oh, don't worry. People always forget the non-alcoholic drink.
> Me: No, it's not that. It's because I can't look at you now after the . . . oh God, I'm so embarrassed . . .
> Him: Why? I said yes.
> Me: You what?
> Him: I said yes. I'd like to do that.

Major problem identified: I couldn't actually talk to men

Oh.

Shit.

I couldn't even ask a man a question. I could barely order an orange juice, let alone commandeer a sexual revolution.

The Lucy in my head and Lucy in real life were gravely misaligned. In my head, I was trailblazing my way into sexy adventure magic. In real life, I was propositioning a guy by demonstrating the symptoms of anaphylactic shock.

The fact I couldn't even talk to a man was a sizable setback to the mission. What was stopping me being able to ask a perfectly nice fella a simple question? You may find this hard to believe, but otherwise I was quite a capable person, able to get through life, even, from time to time, to do things of merit. I was an actress and had performed on West End stages. Speaking was what I did! I'd had books published. I'd travelled. Blimey, when I thought about it, I realised I was calmer getting robbed at knifepoint in Guatemala than I was asking a really lovely bloke if he wanted to do some tantra with me.

It's demoralising to realise during a one-off isolated incident that you're a pillock with the opposite sex. It is doubly dire to realise that this is your modus operandi with the fellas, that this is you in your 'man mode'.

I had never asked a man out before. Oh, sorry, that is complete tosh. I had asked one man out and he rejected me with a text message containing the word 'soz'.

How did I react? Oh, you know, I was cool. I understood.

How did you *actually* react, Lucy? I drank all the booze in the flat, ate approximately a loaf of peanut butter on toast and wailed all night.

Likewise, I had never initiated a first tryst. Well, except on one occasion, but I don't think it counts, as I was a full A4 refill pad to the wind. I was propped up by a bar and slurred the words, 'Shall we kiss?', then lunged at him because I could barely stand or see and definitely couldn't carry out a conversation any more.

So I didn't have a history of asking guys out. I was too terrified that someone would look at me and say, 'God, no, of course not. Why on earth would I want you? What on earth made you think that? What were you thinking?'

Rejection: I was petrified of it.

Arse.

All this was going to be harder than I thought.

A drunk woman, a naked man and a book on tantric sex. What could possibly go wrong?

But this man hadn't rejected me! He wanted to learn tantric sex with me. Where is the caps lock? WAHOO!

How did I proceed? Ask him out for a friendly coffee to discuss how we would do this adult-fun tantric thing? Invite him to mine, open the door to a candlelit room in a robe, and proceed to take him to heaven? Ignore him for a week? Yep, that last one. I was lacking in the confidence department. But all hope wasn't lost. I had my gallant ally in overcoming my innate shyness with men. Tequila.

Although I didn't go in cold on the tequila. I warmed up with some white wine and strong European lager first. Then, as we were both leaving the bar, a mate who had witnessed the whole weeks-long endeavour grabbed me, then got hold of him and barked, 'You two. I can't bear this any more. Kiss. Do something! Anything! NOW!'

So we kissed, and even though it was under duress it was rather nice. Very nice, actually. Oh, how I love kissing. I invited him back to mine and thought we could have a go at the lingam massage from *The Complete Idiot's Guide to Tantric Sex*.

By the way, 'lingam' is the tantric term for penis. Tantra has a whole vocabulary of its own. 'Yoni' is the word for vagina. Pretty, isn't it? It means 'gateway of stars', which is much better than vagina, which actually means 'scabbard/sheath for a sword' or in other words 'somewhere a fella puts his penis'.

I was putting my list into action. My sexual revolution was a-rolling. I had engineered some one-on-one penis time. Go me! Although, wait, what was I thinking? I was drunk and 'lingam massage' basically means 'posh handjob' and I had a handjob phobia.

I wonder whether I'm the only woman who finds handjobs

problematic. They remind me of being a teenager, sitting on some secluded grass in a city centre next to a boy with his jeans around his knees. There's this eager stiff thing in my hand and I don't really have a clue what to do with it. Now I suppose this ineptitude is sweet when you are a teenager, but for a woman in her thirties one starts to think, 'Crikey, Luce, what have you been doing with your time?' In principle, the handjob shouldn't be tricky at all: he has a penis and I have two hands. His penis is sensitive and likes being touched; all I have to do is to touch it in a certain way and it will give him a pleasant experience topped off by an orgasm. What's the problem?

Oh, deary me . . . where are those bullet points? I think handjobs are fraught with bouts of insecurity because:

- Most men are masters at them. They have been practising furiously since about the age of thirteen. As a woman, you can only be shite by comparison.
- You don't have that appendage. You don't have a big keen joystick sticking out the front of you. You can't possibly know what it feels like when it's stroked, yanked or pulled.
- Porn doesn't help. That's all about blowjobs. What about the lost art of handjobs? What if you're not ready to go there with your mouth or you just can't be sure it's clean enough?

So there were a few agonising minutes of me squinting at *The Complete Idiot's Guide to Tantric Sex* while fiddling with a penis and then we both thought *sod it* and had sex. And by sex, I mean 'normal, slightly porny sex'. And by 'normal, slightly porny sex' I mean sex that follows the formula: blowjob, him on top, you on top, bit from behind. He comes. Done.

And yet exploring something different from normal formulaic sex was the very reason I was embarking on my sexy adventure and buying books about tantra on the internet.

My first practical wasn't the sexually pioneering start I'd hoped for. I was finding it all rather challenging, the asking men to get jiggy with me, the taking the lead, the doing things a new way, and my efforts seemed depressingly characterised by some old familiar traits of mine: drunkenness and behaving like a twat.

Major problem identified: I can't get naked with anyone unless I'm drunk

I tried to remember if I had ever had sex, as an adult single person, when I was sober. I thought and thought and thought a bit more. Nope, couldn't think of a single instance of sober sex. And while drunken intercourse was all fair and well, I sensed it didn't really have a place on my Fuckit List.

I'd been getting drunk for years. But at this point in my life I was getting a bit bored of all that came with regular intoxication. The 'Oh tell me I didn't say/do/eat that?' The *hangovers*. Like someone had scooped my brains out and replaced them with an angry man with a hammer. I was once so hung-over I had to get off a bus to regurgitate a poached egg on a busy street. And the self-loathing and shame. I once was so drunk that I slept with someone and I couldn't remember whether we'd used a condom. The next day I had the joyous task of calling him to ask. (We did it three times, he told me. Cheeky. I still don't believe him. We did use a condom, though.)

A friend of mine had stopped drinking four years before. 'I just wanted to see what I could achieve if I wasn't pissed all the time,' he said simply. That really inspired me.

I didn't know whether I wanted to stop drinking entirely, I still enjoyed a Jägerbomb and the odd night of capers, but I didn't want drinking to define me any more. I didn't want to always meet people for drinks; I was starting to think that meeting a friend to sit in a park or watch the sunset would be far preferable to drinking overpriced white wine in yet another hostelry.

If I was to get serious about this sexual adventure, I realised, then booze was going to have a take a back seat, ride in the boot or maybe even get out altogether.

'Normal, slightly porny sex' 101

I should also probably elaborate on what I meant back there, when I said 'normal, slightly porny sex'. In my experience, and I should make it clear here that I haven't had sex with everybody, it goes: bit of fingering, blowjob, him on top, you on top, bit from behind. He comes. Done. Now, there can be a bit of deviation here or there, but this seems to be the general template, which in a way is handy, as it's fail-safe. The satnav is programmed, so you don't really have to think too much. It *is* sex, if you like.

And while 'normal, slightly porny sex' was OK as far as things went, it was never earth-shattering and I rarely, if ever, came. Now, this could have been owing to the perilously high levels of hitherto mentioned drunkenness that tended to be in place when the 'normal, slightly porny sex' occurred. Or it could have been because 'normal, slightly porny sex' always felt a bit more focused on performance rather than pleasure – a sequence of energetic gymnastic exercises rather than a sensuous feast of touch and pleasure.

It would nearly always start with a bit of kissing. You can generally tell how the sexual encounter will be by the kissing. I like soft kisses, with a little bit of tongue and a few nibbles. I like to melt into kissing. But sometimes I would meet people – the tight-lipped kisser, the tongue darter, the flobby dribbler, for example – who I just wasn't kissing-compatible with at all. And while it was inevitable that I wouldn't be well suited sexually with these people, I'd never say, 'Oh no, this kissing isn't working at all, is it? It doesn't bode well, shall we just give up on the adult fun altogether and show each other our favourite comedy clips on YouTube instead?' I'd have sex with them anyway. This is obvious. When you're single you're generally not getting loads of sex and if there is a hunger, you'll take what is on offer if it is vaguely palatable and available.

So the 'normal, slightly porny sex' will start with kissing and then will be hurried up by either:

- A hand in your knickers
- Your hand moved onto his penis

Now, a hand in the knickers doesn't really do it for it me as it misses out the main area where I can be really aroused: my breasts and nipples. If a man spends time touching my breasts and nipples when we're kissing, I will be gloriously aroused, embarrassingly quivery, and then very much ready and looking forward to a hand in the pants. Straight to the knickers is all a bit smear test.

My hand has been moved onto many a penis over the years. And I look back and mourn the fact that I never once responded by saying, 'Thanks, I do know where it is, I'll get there when I'm ready.' But I didn't. To be honest, at the time I never really thought I could or should respond to this, or any of the gripes I had with formulaic sex. I was passive. I'm not proud of it. I just thought this was what sex was. It hadn't dawned on me I could get really involved and start shaping the sex I wanted to have.

Anyway, once the penis was unleashed in these situations it would all become a bit penis-centric, like when a really loud pissed bloke turns up at a party and it all goes a bit 'wey hey, look at me!!'

Now, I know that during 'normal, slightly porny sex' I would give a blowjob, but a man generally wouldn't reciprocate and go down on me. And I'm not sure exactly why this was: whether those men just didn't like doing that, whether they were scared I wasn't clean or that they'd be rubbish, whether they just wanted to get to the shagging, whether I didn't want five minutes of a man randomly noshing my lady place, whether I had a shame about the intimacy of it. The alcohol makes it hard to remember those details. Also, it could have been a bit cultural. You didn't read stories in the tabloids about footballers taking women in a toilet at a club and going down on them, it was always her giving him a blowjob. The blowjob was kinda expected, but reciprocating with cunnilingus wasn't.

And then there was the shagging, which would tend to start with him on top, then move to me on top, and very often get to from behind. But with the shagging, actually with all of it, it would be fast. As though we were trying to get somewhere quickly, like a departure gate when your flight's been called. And I would be manoeuvred around a fair bit, like an IKEA sofa in a new flat. Legs up here, down there. I'd ache in the morning. I'd only ever say 'this is reeeally uncomfortable' if there was a danger I'd break a limb, otherwise I'd be there with my (very unlimber) legs around my ears, tendons screaming, not saying anything. I felt I had to do my part in the performance.

Then he'd come and that would be it, and even though this sex wasn't great for me, I would hope there would be more, in the morning or another time, and I wonder whether this was less because I wanted a replay of the sex, but because not getting any more would mean I had been rejected, it would mean that I had been witnessed totally naked, and then discarded.

So there we have it, 'normal, slightly porny sex' was generally what occurred if I went home with someone for hanky-panky. (Hanky-panky – does it get any better as a phrase?!) It was the norm. The norm wasn't, he puts on a gimp mask, she spanks him with a salad spoon, he comes into a plant pot. Or, he massages her until she orgasms and then asks if he can penetrate her.

'Gasping birds'

Right, where were we? Oh yes, I was trying to learn tantric sex with a chap and failing rather brilliantly. Now, I had thought that there was some magic there with this fella, but then this conversation happened:

On the street. Approximately 11 p.m.

Student night. Think *Shaun of the Dead*, but instead of zombies, drunk teenagers in high shoes lollop past us.

Me: Do you want to come back to mine?
Him: Er, hmmm . . . hmmm . . . I think I should probably stay at mine tonight.
Me: Are you OK?
Him: Yeah . . .
Me: Quick, move over here, that girl looks like she's going to be—
Him: Urghhh.
Me: Sick.
Him: Thanks.
Me: So, tell me. What's up?
(A painful pause)
(This pause is really starting to hurt . . . owwwwww . . . badly)
Him: I'm just having a few doubts, that's all.

Me: Oh.

Him: A bit of a wobble.

Me: Um . . . but well, us learning tantric sex together, it can't really happen if one of us doesn't want to . . . Can it?

Him: Er, no.

So that was that then. But it was fine.

In fact, it was better than fine. I was the leader of my own personal sexual revolution, after all. It was another valuable growth opportunity. I simply smiled and wished him well in a warm and ever so slightly nonchalant manner.

Hmmm, that's not quite what happened, is it, Lucy?

No. I cried on the street. Then I met some friends. Got drunk. Bought a cheeseburger from a chip van and wailed, 'I feel such a plum,' as I ate it on a step.

The next day I lay in bed clutching my head and belching, thinking about how I had cocked it up. I narrowed it down to hundreds of reasons but here are the top five:

1. My body
He saw me naked and thought my bits were weird.

2. My personality
I terrified the poor bloke. I accosted him at a bus stop, told him I'd bought *The Complete Idiot's Guide to Tantric Sex* and asked him if he wanted to learn it with me. Then I ran away and couldn't speak to him for a week. I wanted to explore sex with him, I really really did, but I wasn't used to leading in this way and it made me shy and nervous.

3. My sexual prowess
It was a rubbish handjob. But to be fair, it's hard giving a man a handjob while holding a book.

4. My bedside manner

On our morning together, I did a little fart in bed.* But although it was little I'd been holding it in for some time, so perhaps it was that and something I'd eaten, but whatever it was, that little fart was fierce and when it reached max potency I fully expected gasping birds to come tumbling out of the sky.

5. This sensitive guy with the nice eyes just simply wanted to be with someone better

Clutching my hungover head and debating whether the first step on my journey to discover divine sex had ended because of a fart or a handjob wasn't really what I had in mind when I set off to explore my sexuality.

Nor were those overwhelming and familiar feelings that I wasn't good enough, that I should be better, thinner, quieter, more confident, less mental, more knowledgeable on current affairs, have bigger breasts, that there should be at least one muscle in my bottom . . . I could go on. Forever.

I had so many insecurities and the strange thing was, they felt very old. I think I'd had most of them since I was about eleven or twelve, since I first started thinking about boys. Sometimes I would look in the mirror and be shocked that I was a proper woman, because I felt so very, very young and insecure. I still felt like a little girl who just wanted a boy to like her.

But I was bored of feeling so weak. I wanted to feel strong. Not scarily badass bossy. Just secure in myself. I wanted to be able to ask a man if he wanted to learn tantric sex without having to literally canter away, screaming afterwards. I also very much wanted a man to be able to say, 'I'm just not feeling

---

*I don't normally fart. I don't normally talk about farting. But this one was so epic it demanded space on the page.

it with you,' without me wailing into numerous special-price cocktails. And I wanted to stop being such a bitch to myself. I didn't have the time for all this self-flagellation: I had a sexual revolution to be getting on with And I had a sneaky feeling that I wouldn't be able to have beautiful sex until I felt beautiful. And I didn't think feeling properly beautiful meant cutting my hair or losing a stone or a guy telling me I was fit. I thought it would probably have to come from me loving what I'd already got.

LEARNING TO LOVE MYSELF

Now there's a chapter heading. I used to wince and pull a comedy gurning face when confronted with those words. 'Love yourself? What a load of wanky bollocks.'

At the time I'm writing about, I was living in a flat-share in Brighton with some friends. 'The vegans', my mum used to call them. She was fascinated by the vegans. 'They have to eat eggs!' she'd say triumphantly, in the middle of a conversation about something else entirely. The vegans were lovely. One of them, Simon, was an old friend, a boyfriend from eons ago. He was acquainted with pretty much every self-help book ever written. Buddha in the Bedroom Next Door, I called him. His is an inspiring story. He grew up on a rough estate, got into crime, went to prison, came out, turned his life around, became an actor, personal trainer and everyday guru. From burglar to Buddha. Literally.

Experiencing a dumping in Vegan Headquarters was completely unlike experiencing a dumping anywhere else. They didn't drink, for starters, so there wasn't one single 'God, what a wanker' discussion over gin. Instead conversations like this happened.

Me: I'm such a twat. He dumped me.
Buddha in the Bedroom Next Door: This is such an amazing gift for you.
Me: Huh?

Or:

BBND: What are you thinking about the situation?
Me: Huh?
BBND: Your focus creates your reality. Where is your focus?
Me: Huh?
BBND: Acknowledge your thoughts.

'Acknowledge your thoughts' turned out to be a biggie. He wandered off to check on his rice and I sat there trying to do what he'd said, to acknowledge my thoughts. Current thought activity was bubbling away like this:

It must be my vagina. I'm a freak with a mutant vagina. I bet sensitive guy with the nice eyes didn't want to have beautiful, mind-blowing sex with me because I've got a weird vagina. I bet it's really, really odd. Oh God, maybe it smelled. I am so disgusting.

Or it really could have been that fart I did in bed. I mean, I am fascinated by the extraordinary strength of that fart. But he might have thought they were normal. He probably thought farts of such magnitude were always phff-ing out of my bottom.

Clearly, I will never have sex again. I'm going to eat cheese. I hate rejection; I love cheese. Brilliant, that's all I need, a cheese obsession. Oh, maybe it was my feet that put him off. I am so foul. It is astonishing that anyone has ever had sex with me. Argh! We don't have any cheese. I live with vegans . . .

There was a constant stream of it. Up to that moment I had thought I was a bit of a hippy, into peace and love, you know, didn't hate anything. Turned out I was meaner than anyone I'd ever come across – to myself.

Once I started noticing it, I couldn't stop noticing it. Over the next days, here and there, I would catch my thoughts. Rather than letting my internal dialogue spill all over the shop unchecked as I usually did, I would stop and have a look at what I was saying to myself. There was hardly a ten-minute window in my day when I wasn't having a go at myself. 'God, you're so fat, Lucy.' 'Wow, you look shit.' Blah blah blah it went. 'Oh God, your skin is so disgusting,' or, 'Look at the bags under your eyes,' or, 'Lucy, sort your face out.' The word 'disgusting' came up again and again. Sometimes I'd swap it for 'revolting'.

The more I was aware of it the more exhausted I became with it. This venom had been in my head my whole life. Although, it wasn't my *whole* life, was it? I hadn't been born thinking this stuff. I wasn't saying it at nursery or singing it at Brownies. But I'd picked it up from somewhere, and it had been firmly strapped in by the time I was thirteen. Thirteen was the age when I stopped wanting to eat and lost a lot of weight. Also the age when I sat for a whole evening just looking in the mirror and crying. I suppose I was thirteen when I turned from being a girl into a young woman. It wasn't a pleasant initiation into womanhood, more a realisation that how I looked was a monumentally big deal.

Where had it come from? My mum didn't sit there telling me I was foul, my teachers didn't repeatedly point out that as a woman I should be decorative, slim and pretty. And yet I wholeheartedly knew this to be true, and had spent the majority of my life repeatedly berating myself for falling short.

Society and culture told me again and again that women and girls should be pretty. It was there in fairy tales and pantomimes, where the princesses were always beautiful, and beauty meant goodness, ugliness evil. In the endless diet books and exercise videos that I saw, in my house and others', in the way food was often 'naughty' – 'Ooo, I shouldn't really eat that, but just one,' 'Oh, go on then, the diet starts tomorrow.' In girls' and women's magazines that offered only pictures of pretty, slim, white girls and women. In the adverts for tights, bicycles, cars, cat food, men's deodorant. The pictures of women showing their bottoms or boobs that were pinned up in offices, in teenage boys' bedrooms, or hidden behind packets of peanuts in pubs. Perhaps I picked it up from the way I would hear men comment on women: 'God, look at the state of her,' 'She's a big girl,' 'You'd have to drink until she was pretty.' Or the way women commented on women: 'What on earth is she wearing?' Or put themselves down: 'I'm so fat,' 'I hate my arms.' There was also a big picture of a topless sixteen-year-old in the *Sun* every day. The more I think about it, the sadder I feel for the little girl faced with a naked ideal image of how she was supposed to look every day, there with the news of the day, the sport, the TV guide and 'Dear Deidre', which my mum liked. Maybe it was in the rows of porn magazines that would be on the shelves in newsagents. Or maybe it was just the whole sodding lot.

I'd never unlearned any of this, or challenged it. Instead I simply accepted that I fell short of the ideal expected of me, and hated myself for it. I don't say that lightly: I loathed myself. At least it made some sense of the fact that I hated my body so much that I needed to be bolloxed on booze in order to get naked, and heaped such scorn on myself when I was rejected.

It was even more demoralising to acknowledge that I was part of the problem. I had rampantly perpetuated all this for years. I'd moaned about my body and face in front of young women and girls, including my nieces and goddaughters. I'd written characters who hated their bodies. I had just absorbed it all as 'normal'.

It now seemed glaringly obvious that I couldn't get anywhere near the great nooky I was hankering after if I was riddled with hatred for the very body I was nookying with. I felt as though I was waking up and I hadn't even been aware I was fast asleep. The internal harangue that criticised me was still going on and on as it had done for years, but another voice had started to fight back. It would rage and roar: 'Nooooooooooo!! I'm not doing this any more!'

Body image – a bright light is switched on

Once I turned the light on, it got worse, much worse, before it got better. I had to face just how ugly I found myself.

I referred to my body as 'a festival of female shitness', seeing my flaws as 'many and mighty'. You might want to look away, but here is a quick rundown of the sort of things I was saying to myself about myself.

I have thin limp hair, like a damp Poundstretcher mop. I am going grey. But, to my frustration, the process of going grey is slow and maverick; you don't wake up one day as a distinguished silver fox, rather you rise, look in the mirror and realise you have one grey badger stripe and four strands of white hair, three inches in length, which stick up vertically.

Moving down to my face . . . random picked spot somewhere on my chin, a bit of a man-moustache going on, bags under my eyes so I look a bit like an elephant, raised red scar on chin, lopsided jaw, wide moon cheeks, two random moley things with hairs coming out them, yellow teeth and one grey/black one. I'm sure there's more. Oh yes, my wrinkles! Deep smile lines either side of my mouth and frown lines in between and at the corners of my eyes. Oh and lots of dark spots of skin or random red patches of skin. The general sense that the whole façade is simply sagging, crumbling, decomposing into my treble-chinned neck.

Fat arms, fat fingers, make that crooked fat fingers, feet that are actually quite a nice shape, but suffer from a weird fungal foot problem that makes them very hot and, especially in cheap footwear, which I've always been partial to, a bit stinky.

Huge nipples, stretch marks on my boobs, one breast is bigger than the other, they both like to swing out to my armpits.

My bottom is large like a big telly. It has the consistency of a budget beanbag. And if I stop dancing suddenly while not wearing tights, realistically it can take up to seven seconds before it stops moving. You would never see my bottom selling pants, or tights, or beer, or aftershave, or pilchards. A women's magazine would never feature my arse in a pair of shorts, running across a beach, with the caption 'Be a Man Magnet'. You would never see my bottom in a men's mag or a tabloid newspaper. The only time you might see a bottom like mine would be with a big red circle around it and the words 'Weight-Gain Nightmare' or 'Cellulite Hell Shocker'

Oh, and I have more pubic hair than seems necessary or fair. I do try to make it hospitable but frequently it's found trespassing on the tops of my legs. I also have a few grey pubic hairs.

It wasn't all bad though, like I say, I thought my feet were quite a nice shape. And sometimes, say after a bout of diarrhoea, I quite liked my stomach.

On some level I knew that it was 'what's inside that counts'. I had heard that phrase uttered from time to time. But if we learn by repetition, and we become what we see, then I had been bombarded by the notion that I wasn't attractive enough and I needed to do something about myself, in particular by buying products to make me less of an eyesore.

And there were so many bits one could buy! The more I thought about it, the more utterly bonkers it all seemed. Take serums, for example. One can buy an anti-ageing serum, a beauty serum, a youth-activating serum, a facial-radiance serum, a firming serum, a vitamin-C serum, an anti-wrinkle serum, a lifting serum, a repairing serum, a micro serum, a youth-boost facial serum, a double serum, a hydrating serum, a pro serum, an antioxidant serum, a cellular serum, an intensive serum. Ask most blokes what a serum is and they won't have a sodding clue. Then clarify for them that it is a potion for the face that goes on after the cleanser and the toner and before the moisturiser, night cream and eye cream at night or before the make-up in the day, and by make-up I mean the primer, the foundation, the concealer, the luminising powder, the . . . I don't know about you, but I'm starting to wonder if someone is having a laugh.

Only it's more sinister than funny. Because it's not just items that are being flogged to me, but procedures. How about a filler injected under the skin of my face, or into my lips, or maybe some infrared light, radio frequency, ultrasound or some needles to traumatise my face, or bacteria that causes botulism injected into my facial muscles, or maybe I'm best taking a few layers of skin off. Or for the right cash, a surgeon could cut the skin of my breast, pop an implant in it and stitch the breast back up. Or he could surgically transfer some of my fat from my bum to my boobs or face. Or I could have 'a facelift for the vagina'.

Or what about the Mummy Makeover – a tummy tuck, boob job and liposuction combo costing approximately £10,000.

Although hang about, the adverts that are flashing up REPEATEDLY as I research this say there is a 0 per cent finance option. So I don't even have to let having no money stop me from having a fella cut me up and make me perfect. Lucy, that's rather sexist, women can be surgeons too. Yes, but there don't seem to be many of them, at least not what I can see from the plastic surgery companies online. I do a quick search and find an article on Racked that cites the stat that 92 per cent of surgeries are performed on women, while women only make up 15 per cent of the doctors. There is something a bit eerie about it. Clothed male doctors get rich by cutting up naked women to make them 'perfect'.

So I couldn't really blame myself; a few years of seeing the adverts for all these products, treatments and procedures would probably make most women and girls feel utterly terrible about themselves. The adverts are on billboards, buses, tubes, trains, in supermarkets, high streets, on the radio. And don't forget the screens. These adverts love screens. They will be all over the telly and 'puter too. 'Dull, dry and lifeless hair? Unsightly pores/ stretchmarks?' they might ask. 'Who doesn't want better skin?' Or, 'Dull, blotchy, uneven skin?' Or they will tell you to 'Break the cycle of oily roots and dry ends' or to 'Fight signs of ageing!' You should be flawless, voluminous, triple hydrated.

And then there are the magazines, which back all this up with front-page features like 'Beach Body Fast', 'Tone Every Zone', '775 Ways to Nail Your Party Look', 'Shape Issue Fashion for Every Figure', 'Work It Longer Legs', 'Leaner Lines; Sexier Silhouette', 'How to Do Dazzling Evening Make-Up', 'The Real Beauty Secrets of the Stars.' Even if you don't buy them you will see them, on shelves and at tills, at the doctor's or the dentist's or in a café, and they will be advertised, too, on telly and screens. Oh, and don't forget that they, in turn, will have more adverts in them. Teams upon teams of people are employed to make sure that all these messages, these adverts for products and procedures, these little suckers WILL FIND YOU.

The business of perfection is a nightmare. I've only picked a tiny corner of the big, scabby mess here. How do you even play all this? Medicate? Scream? Punch someone? I'm surprised lots of young women aren't starving themselves, hating themselves, cutting themselves . . . oh, hang about.

And that was what made me saddest. I thought back to myself as a young woman and my own experiences of starving myself, and about my friends and their experiences with body image, and the eating disorders that we all had to varying degrees. And then I realised that it's still the same, if not worse, for the young women who are coming after us. All that brain time spent comparing ourselves and hating ourselves. What a waste. What would we be capable of if we weren't inheriting all this as normal?

I realised that since my young teens I had been at war with myself. Losing a war with myself. Actually, this war analogy is crap, because nothing was opposing the hatred. No, it was more like I'd been under the rule of an evil dictator who thought that all women should be slim and beautiful and reminded its subjects constantly.

Loving my bum

Having acknowledged my thoughts, it became evident that I was dissatisfied with pretty much all of me. Some bits, however, were 'wronger' than others. My bum for example, was MAJORLY wrong. It didn't take me long to stumble across this age-old revulsion towards my own bottom.

At the time, I needed new jeans. I needed new jeans because my arse was literally hanging out of my old ones. When I put my jeans on, I had to bend over with my head between my legs and check that no pubic hairs were peeping out of the gaping holes in my jeans. I wore long jumpers over these jeans, and was careful not to be followed upstairs. I really needed a new pair of jeans. However, there was a problem. I HATED BUYING JEANS. I had tried to buy jeans not long before, but the mission had been unsuccessful. I'd gone to Selfridges, cried in the changing rooms and asked Twitter for help.

I didn't understand jeans. I still don't. We are obese as a nation. If you believe the papers, we're the fattest people in Europe, the world, we're fatter than the sumos. And all I want to know is this: if we are so mahooosive, then why are we making jeans that only a teenage girl with an eating disorder could wear? Why is it so hard to find a piece of denim that covers your arse without making you want to cry?

Anyway, I sat down on the floor in the lounge at Vegan Headquarters one morning. We did have chairs and furniture and stuff, but for such a long time we hadn't had chairs and furniture and stuff that we mostly still used the floor. As I sat down I said something along the lines of: ''Scuse me! Holes in jeans scenario, divert your gaze from my massive bottom. I need to get new jeans, but it's traumatic when you've got an arse like mine.'

Nothing unremarkable about that really. Very common Lucy chat. Except I was trying to love myself and these words jarred, partly because slagging off my own bottom felt so familiar.

'I hate my bum,' 'I hate my bum,' 'I hate my bum' . . .

I'd been saying this again and again for years and years and years.

It was not surprising at all that I loathed my bum. I had seen a lot of images of what a woman's bottom should look like, and my huge two-tier cellulite and stretch-mark collage bore no resemblance to any of them. But I didn't want to hate anything about myself now. I was knackered by all the hating. And I couldn't see the bottom hatred working out well on my sexual journey. How could I let go and have great sex if I kept apologising for how I looked? How could I be free to move and explore my sexuality if I very much hoped that he, she or they didn't catch sight of my behind?

So, I tried to turn it around and see the positive in my derrière. I became conscious of some pretty cool facts about this particular part of me. For a start, my bottom may not be small but it is really, really comfy. I sat on it through school and university; I've sat on it in all sorts of different countries; I've sat on it to write books, to watch people get married, to hold newborn babies.

Come to think of it, there was nothing I hadn't done without my bum there like a soft cushion behind me should I need it to sit. And I couldn't think of one time when my bum was ever cold. So it was time to whisper, 'Hey Squidgy Bottom, sorry I've been such a cow, can we just forget all about that and move on? Thank you for being such a great bum, I love you.' And, yes, I did catch myself thinking, 'Oh, Luce, you are such a twat.' But the fact I was harsh on myself for being kind to myself made me more determined than ever to turn all this hatred around.

Loving my boobs

I also thought about my boobs. It's hard to know what to call 'boobs' when you write about them. Buddha in the Bedroom Next Door called them Bobbies, I think after Bobby Davro. This has suddenly gone weird, hasn't it? Anyway, my breasts. My poor breasts.

'I hate my boobs.' I'd repeated this phrase so many times over the years. But spilling hate on my breasts wasn't as comedy as hating my big bottom. The fact I hadn't loved my boobs for years made me feel sad. Because I could pinpoint exactly when the hate, or shame, started.

Blimey, I'd been ashamed of my breasts since they first arrived.

I remember being eleven. It was after a ballet class, and I was having a shower. I looked down at my newly emerging boobies, and saw some red scratches on them. I thought I'd just scratched myself slightly as I washed. But that night the scratches hadn't gone. And they were still there in the morning. I was terrified. It looked as though angry claws had taken a swipe at me. I now know that they were stretch marks and they do eventually fade. But the eleven-year-old me didn't have a clue what was going on. What I did know was that I wasn't normal. My older brother would bring the *Sun* newspaper home from work, and the girls on Page 3 didn't have these marks. I was a freak. I was a failure. I was horrible. I definitely couldn't tell anyone. I was too ashamed.

This marked the beginning of a really complex and sad relationship with my breasts. As a teenager I didn't want to reveal them to the boys I went out with (unless it was very dark and I'd had a lot of 20/20), but amid all this shame, I was learning that they loved being touched. WOWZERS. HOW THEY LOVED BEING TOUCHED! My nipples were fabulously sensitive. Having my nipples played with was . . . well . . . yes, please, more.

Yet, in bed with fellas, I'd always felt, 'Oh, the poor bloke, he must hate my breasts. He must wish he was with someone with much nicer boobs.' And if a man didn't spend much time with my breasts during sex, I'd never suggest that he did, I'd never tell him that I was really sensitive there, I assumed he didn't want to go near my breasts because they were so disgusting.

It got me thinking. We'd done something a bit weird with boobs, I reckoned. Because while it seemed as though boobs were everywhere, they were there purely for the titillation of men. And I guess I had just assumed that this is what my boobs were there for too. It felt a bit to me like we women didn't actually own our boobs any more – the men did. And the weird thing was I don't think men even wanted to own our boobs. The media and online porn industry had just given them our breasts. And us women hadn't even noticed. But suddenly it was like we'd (well, I'd) woken up from a doze on the sofa and gone, 'Jeeeezz, what the frickin' hell is going on with our boobs?'

And what had gone on with our boobs? I don't even know where to start. Naked teenage breasts were in our daily family newspapers. Padded bras were being made for primary-school girls and sold in Tesco. Breast-augmentation surgery for purely cosmetic reasons was on the rise each year. Sorry, you're probably in an advanced state of decomposition by now. But there's just so much to say about BOOBS!

But surely breasts have some bigger and better functions than just making men go, 'Cor, look at the tits on that.' (THAT! THAT! I'd never even noticed the use of the word 'that' instead of 'her'.) Let's just take a moment to consider some of the wonderful things that breasts can do. For one thing, breasts feed babies. Don't get me started on this. It's frickin' awesome! That alone makes the Bobby Davros rock. And there was another point which I thought was rather wonderful. I found it out in a book. It was this: breasts are a woman's sexual hotspot. Positive sexual pole, I think the tantra term is. A man's positive sexual pole is, guess what? Yep, the willy. Oh, I do love the word 'willy', it's right up there with 'bosom'. OK. So a man's positive sexual pole is the willy. But for the woman it's the breasts, which, rather beautifully, is also where the heart is. It's not downstairs, which made sense as to why if men went straight there at sexy time, I found it all a bit uncomfortable and nothing-y. But when you stimulate these positive sex poles, the penis and the breasts, arousal gathers and spreads around the rest of the body and the good times roll.

It all felt a bit bloomin' strange. Breasts were everywhere, yet I'd only just found out this golden nugget of information about breasts from a book about tantra I'd ordered off the internet.[1]

Anyway. I finally cupped my breasts and said, after thirty-five years: 'Hey boobs, I love you. You are amazing, and so beautifully sensitive. I promise I'll be a bit kinder going forward.'

Not saying 'I'm such a twat' any more

There was some major refurbishment going on in my brain, which was both seismic and necessary. The way I had behaved with the tantric fella – the hyperventilating questions, the alcohol for courage, the complete meltdown post-dumping – had scared me and I wanted to get to a point where this wouldn't happen again.

It wasn't just that I lambasted my body and its various compartments, I berated my actual self too. One trait I noticed was that I often followed or preceded many of my utterances with the words, 'I'm such a twat.' Yep, 'I'm such a twat.' I said it a lot. But why would I do that? I mean, yes, OK, fair dues, I could be a plum from time to time. But what was with me *constantly* putting myself down? Why did I devalue myself in this way? I wouldn't say it about someone else; I didn't even think I'd speak so disparagingly about an inanimate object.

I did more detailed personal put-downs too. For instance, I might undermine my achievements: someone would say, 'Oh, you've had books published?' and I'd elaborate with, 'Oh, yes, just chick lit, I won't win any Man Bookers,' laugh, laugh. They might then say, 'But it's very hard to get published,' and I would follow up with, 'Oh, I've just been really lucky.' Or I might hear, 'Oh, you're an actress!' and I would respond with, 'Well, I've really only played tiny parts.' A compliment on my ability would be trumped with, 'I know absolutely nothing except what star signs people are compatible with really.' Sorry, it's all a bit puke-making, isn't it?

Why oh why did I do this? Was I terrified of being big-headed? That could well have been something to do with it. I did go to a Catholic convent school, which taught me blessed are the meek and humble, not 'you're awesome, badass, sing it, sister'. The only version of a mature, empowered, confident-in-her-sexuality woman they offered me was the Virgin Mary. Sorry, hang about. I need to just look at that sentence again. Oh bollocks.

Or had I absorbed the 'bring 'em down' culture we have in the British press to such an extent that I would bring myself down first to circumvent anyone doing it for me? By 'bring 'em down' culture, I mean the way it seems that one moment a woman is great, beautiful, and the next she's shamed herself somehow, let herself go, got too fat, too thin, taken drugs, and she gets snatched down from the pedestal. The tabloid media are fascinated by and obsessed with showing every step of this fall from grace, any weight gain, occasions of too much booze or drugs, a bad case of fake tan.

Sometimes I wished I was American. They're always wanging on about radical self-love and the like. But here in Britain we don't do that, do we? I don't know about you, but I use self-deprecation because it's funny and endearing and no one likes a show-off. If I dared to be all, 'I'm totally fine with how I am,' I'd be afraid that people might say, 'She's a bit full of herself, that one. She's up her own arse.' They might take the piss and pray I'd fall flat. In Britain I think a lot of us are stuck in this tragicomic routine of putting ourselves down all the time.

To some extent, we create our own reality. Our thoughts and words have the power to shape events. As proven by the fact that if I'm walking up the stairs with a full glass and think, 'I'm going to spill this,' within seconds I'll be needing the kitchen roll. People swear by affirmations: Olympians visualise themselves perfectly executing manoeuvres and then standing victorious on podiums. The mind is a powerful place. Mine was housing a very chatty bird who was intent on destroying me. Great.

All this hatred had been there for years; I knew I wasn't going to dismantle it straight away. But I was trying, trying to love my physical bits, and also the actual *me* of me, too.

Getting back out there

After all these months of unpicking the reasons for my bumblefuckery, I decided to get back in the 'picking up men for sexual educational purposes' saddle and tried my luck at internet dating. I wrote a pithy profile and picked a flattering photo. She was off!

I was quickly communicating with a man, the stuff that dreams are made of. He was hilarious. A writer. I was a writer. Made for each other, we were! His messages made me giddy like a girl, or a lamb, liable to skip or giggle at any moment, when I wasn't fretting about what I should wear on our first date, that is. Because we soon decided to go on a date!

Everyone I knew offered me the same piece of sage moral counsel. 'IT'S A FIRST DATE. DON'T, WHATEVER YOU DO, GET DRUNK OR KISS HIM!' So I went on said date, consumed four pints of strong European lager, three shots of a dark liquor that tasted slightly worse than, but not dissimilar to, grappa, and snogged him outside a pub. I did wake up alone in my own bed the next day, however, but that isn't something I am particularly proud of, as I was fully clothed, with a Nutella sandwich stuck to my bottom.

There were many disappointing aspects to this situation, the main one being – and I'm really ashamed to say this, it's really shitty, I am warning you – that I snogged him but I hadn't really wanted to snog him. Yeah, pretty pathetic, isn't it? For all involved. We had been getting on well, we were having a laugh, and he went for a kiss, and I kissed him back because . . . oh, why did I decide to write a bloomin' book about all this?! OK, just say it, Luce: I snogged him because I didn't want to spoil the atmosphere. I didn't want to ruin the 'let the good times roll' vibe by saying, 'Whoa! What do you think you're playing at, sunshine? I'm not snogging you, definitely not yet and maybe not ever!'

Now, don't get me wrong. I love snogging. And he was a nice guy. I didn't mind that I snogged the fella, as such. I had kissed far, far, less suitable people. I was just weirded out by the fact that when he went in for that first kiss, I didn't want to. I thought it was too soon, far too soon, to be on the lips-up, but I did it anyway.

And it's not the first time I've obliged a man who has gone in for a kiss at an oddly premature moment.

Once, a fella lunged in for the first kiss while I was telling him one of my favourite stories about how my mum ran the London marathon. I was talking. He should have been riveted.

Another time, a bloke lunged in for the first snog at some traffic lights. It was late afternoon in central London and we were about to cross the road and go to a café for our first date. I wasn't even looking at him. I was looking at the road I was about to cross.

It's not like I have any particular rules on when the first kiss should be. I don't really have rules on anything. I'm not a religion. But if at all possible I like a little sense of occasion about it, and I really like there to be a bit of anticipation. I enjoy the bit-twitching build-up before the first kiss. I like looking in someone's eyes and feeling an 'ey up, what's going on down there?' stirring. I like daydreaming about kissing them as I get to know them, I like feeling all that glorious sexy energy build, so that when I do feel his lips touch mine for the first time, it's sublime.

So, the thing that annoys me about all these premature kisses is that they were that – they were kisses.

Because rather than saying, 'Oh, no, let's wait and kiss somewhere else, maybe under the stars or at least in the vicinity of a tree,' or, 'Can we at least wait until I've FINISHED MY FASCINATING STORY ABOUT MY MOTHER RUNNING THE MARATHON!' or, 'I'm not sure I'm ready to kiss you yet, it doesn't feel right,' I didn't say anything at all. I just kissed these men.

And that made me want to stand up, clench my fists and make this sound: 'EEEUUURRRRRRGGGGHHHHHHH!'

Because situations where I was doing stuff with men that I didn't really want to were rubbish for me and really rubbish for them.

So there I was, feeling a bit disturbed and ashamed about this. Normally the episode would have simply have been filed under 'Lucy being a plonker with the opposite sex', an already bulging folder, and I would have got on with doing stuff. Ah ha ha, but I was living with the vegans, in particular with Buddha in the Bedroom Next Door. And sorry little episodes didn't get sneakily filed away, not when he was around. Buddha in the Bedroom Next Door heard the story. He frowned.

'Show me the profile thing you put up on this site.'

So I did. Now, in my defence, it wasn't a bad profile. Lots of fellas wrote to me. Some said it was funny and refreshing.

I watched Buddha in the Bedroom Next Door's face as he read it. He pursed his lips, furrowed his brow and set his chin back in his neck so it looked like he had mumps. I didn't sense he was feeling my funny freshness.

He finished reading and did three perfect squats.

Buddha: So the bloke you snogged had read this about you?
Me: Hmmm.
Him: *(Three more squats)* Did you mention your sexual mission thing?
Me: Nope.
Him: *(Three more squats. Touches his toes for approximately ten seconds. Stands upright.)* You see, the thing is, Luce . . . *(A long dramatic pause)* if you communicate half of yourself, you'll attract half of yourself.

Me: Huh?

Him: If you are not clear on who you are and what you want, how can you expect the other person to hear the real you?

Me: Wha—?

Him: If you don't communicate your truth, you'll attract a lie. I'm going to the loo, might be a while. *(He winces)* Always happens after a juice fast.

Me: *(Whispering to myself because he's gone)* Wow.

I sat up in bed and thought about what he'd just said. It generally took me at least a few minutes to fathom what he was on about. On one occasion it took nearly three weeks. But today's stuff went straight into the vein.

If you communicate half of yourself, you'll attract half of yourself.

I had communicated half of myself on this dating profile. I knew I had. I'd communicated the drunken, jokey half of myself. Of course I had, that's what you do in England. But . . . blimey. There was a lot more to me than just being someone who got drunk all the time.

If I was honest, I didn't want to meet a man who got pissed all the time. I wanted to meet a man who was up for bigger and better adventures than sitting in a pub all night, like travelling to new places and making each other's bodies sing.

That was what I wanted. But my profile had no hint of any of this. My dating profile was a big old fart of a lie and I got the date that my drunken jokey lie of a profile dictated. It was pretty obvious when I thought about it.

It made me wonder. What if I'd answered all those questions really honestly? Would I have met a man who felt the same as me? It also made me wonder when I'd start doing all this stuff right. I couldn't help but think that I was majorly flunking sex school.

It emerges I have a bit of a problem communicating with the fellas

Something was occurring to me and it wasn't fetching. I had a rummage through my relationship history to see what had been going on and, whoa, what had been going on had actually been going on and, on and on and bleeding on. *Repeatedly.*

I'd been making the same mistake over and over with greater and greater intensity for years and years and years. Nice one, Luce. Yes, as I riffled through my apocalyptic relationship history, one fact kept rearing its not particularly pretty head.

I had always been afraid to really talk to the men in my life about how I was feeling or what I wanted and needed.

It appeared over and over and over again. Me at sixteen not wanting to snog a boy, but snogging him anyway because I didn't like to say 'no'. Why? Because I didn't like to ruin the atmosphere, because I didn't want to upset him. Then, me at thirty-*sodding*-five doing the exact same thing! Me at all different ages with boyfriends, knowing that they weren't right for me, knowing that deep down I needed to leave, but being too scared to say the words, being too scared to upset them.

I remember once I was spending a few days with this guy I was seeing, and he'd planned some lovely bits for us to do, picnics, outings and the like. But I had been asked to write two newspaper articles, and doing them would encroach on our time together. It was important for me to write them; it was a great opportunity for me. All I needed to do was clearly say: 'I need to set aside some hours while I am with you to write. This very exciting opening has come up for me.' It sounds so EASY!!! But I got myself into a right tizz at the thought of telling him that. I was almost paralysed at the thought of it. In the end I got up more or less in the middle of the night to do the articles. I could hardly keep my eyes open for the picnic. I was so used to doing what guys wanted that I found it virtually impossible to speak up.

Scared to speak. Scared to speak. Again and again.

And I think I found it so hard to say to men what I was really feeling or ask for what I needed because I'd not really seen other women do it.

I know what you're thinking. You're thinking, 'That theory's so hardcore it needs a guitar solo after it . . .'

I'll elaborate a bit. My parents are the most incredible people on the planet. They have been married a gazillion years (well, fifty-six). They are happy together, but my father is, hmmm, how to say it, he is the head, the king of the relationship. We might think of it now as a 1950s relationship; Mum looks after him, and he supports her financially. It is the same set-up as countless other couples. This was pretty much the norm for the relationships I grew up watching closely and those that were presented to me in popular culture. Predominantly what I saw was women making men's lives easier, often at the expense of their own needs.

The woman as the supportive housewife has been a powerful female archetype in recent generations. Newspapers in the first half of the twentieth century often had regular 'Advice to Wives' or 'How to Keep a Husband' columns, full of ways in which women should tailor their own behaviour to flatter the male ego. Nowadays, us girls are supposedly equal to men. But it's still so *new*. It's only a hundred years now since we got the vote. It takes time, and generations, to shift ideologies that have been in place for thousands of years. No wonder I had been finding it hard to say, 'No, I don't want to do that/snog you/have that sort of sex,' etc.

Whatever happens, I vowed, I need to start speaking truthfully to men. I even got a henna tattoo on Brighton Pier, the Chinese symbol for 'truth', on my right wrist. That wasn't even the scariest bit. The scariest bit was that quite often, in public, I jumped my legs wide apart like a hobbit, held up my right wrist, and shouted, 'It's all about speaking the truth, man!'

Shaping the sex I had

This being scared to speak was doubly present when it came to sex. And I began to think that it wasn't just me who had this problem.

The more curious, fascinated and passionate I became about the subject of sex and, in particular, female sexuality, the more I talked about it to people. And there was something I started to hear regularly, particularly from young women when they described to me the sex they were having. It was the same phrase, or near enough, again and again: 'I don't know what is wrong with me, but it really hurts.'

Always the mention of pain and always the self-blame. While this saddened me it didn't altogether surprise me. It resonated with experiences I'd had over the years. Having sex with a sense of 'I'm supposed to be enjoying this', rather than feelings of 'Oooeee, I'm enjoying this!' I remembered times I had endured pain, and rather than stopping proceedings, I carried on, hoping he'd change position or finish soon. Sometimes I even acted as though I was enjoying things I wasn't.

Why would I do that? Why would I allow someone to physically hurt me and pretend I was enjoying it? Well, I think there were a few things at work here. For a start, I wanted the guy to like me. He was enjoying himself and I wanted to be this great woman who made him happy. I thought it was more important that he enjoyed himself than I did. But also I felt sure that I was *supposed* to be enjoying it. And here we are, back at porn again. I had seen this sort of sex, this sort of 'banging', in porn. Whether real or feigned, the women always seemed to enjoy it, so I should too. This was the script.

Although maybe the real problem was that women in porn don't have much of a script. I definitely hadn't heard a woman say, 'That hurts, could you slow down please,' or, 'I'm not ready yet, I'm not aroused enough,' in porn. No wonder I hadn't been able to find the words. It was up to me to find my own script and change my own story. Oh crikey. I felt sure this wouldn't be easy for me. But I felt equally sure it was going to be blooming necessary.

So, I had a think about how I could create a new script for myself when it came to sex with the menz. I couldn't be sure whether I'd be able to put it into actual practice, but I figured thinking about it beforehand could only help. Here's what I thought I would try:

1) To be far more upfront about sex in general. To be open with guys about my sex mission, tell them before any sexy shenanigans what I'm looking for, e.g. slow sex rather than random drunken bonking. I figured the more I could say beforehand the better. Much easier to say in conversation that I wanted to experience really slow sex than to wait until a guy was trying to insert a penis somewhere.

2) If an incident of adult fun was on the cards, say beforehand what I would be up for, e.g. 'Just to say, I'm not ready to have sex with you tonight, but it would be lovely to have a little fully clothed smooch.'

3) Have some phrases in a stockpile so that, should I find myself in my birthday suit with a chap and things start to move too quickly, I won't blurt out, 'Slow down, you randy goat,' or more likely – and worse – think, 'Slow down, you randy goat,' but not say anything. Such phrases might include: 'The thing that most turns me on is going reeeeally slow.' 'I don't

enjoy sex unless it starts really slow.' 'I'm not ready for that yet. Let's kiss some more.' 'Let's slow down. There's no rush.'
4) I would also really make an effort to express when I liked something. To say, 'Oh that feels amazing when you touch me there.' And to allow myself to be vocal in my pleasure.

I wondered how it would be for guys who weren't used to women asking for the touch and sex that they wanted. I imagined that if handled well, it would be relaxing for the man to know that what he was giving the woman was what she really wanted.

It struck me that I, and, I would hazard, other women, had somehow bought into a belief that men would just know how to pleasure me and wouldn't need any schooling in how I liked my sexing at all. It was like a myth had been fed to me that men were sexual masters. My experiences of having sex with men certainly didn't bear this out, yet still this weird notion lolled about in my mind. Yet again I'd come up against a strong belief about sex I didn't even know I had, but which I was going to have a good go at getting rid of.

SLOW SEX – GETTING THE HANG OF IT NOW

Gatecrashing a road trip with two handsome German men

There is a game drunk people play where you put your forehead on the end of a long pole – a broom handle, for example – then, with the other end of the broom on the ground, you run round and round ten times. Then you toss the stick away and run, or try to, generally veering across the lawn and landing on your arse. Let's use that as the metaphor for me in the early stages of my sex mission.

But it did slowly improve. In fact, the day after the date where I snogged the fella when I hadn't really wanted to, I met someone rather exciting, someone I fancied the pants off, and he turned out to be instrumental in the slow sex quest. But, of course, it didn't start smoothly, oh ho no, we had to get through him telling me I repelled him and the worst handjob in the world before things started looking up.

It was an unusual scenario, really. I didn't meet this fella in a café, bar, on the internet or the back of a newspaper. I gatecrashed his holiday. Gatecrashing hot men's holidays was not something I did often, I was far too timid, but a friend had sort of decided that I should go on this road trip with her two male friends, because she thought I would get along with said chap.

(I reeeally owe her dinner.) So that was how I ended up driving a car from Switzerland to Mallorca with two German blokes. For the sake of this story we'll call them Dark-Haired German and Light-Haired German. Behold my powers of description and quake.

Hitherto I had thought that German men were into long sausages and porn. Oh, how wrong I was. These fellas seemed to be into, OK, this is going to seem weird, communication. Yes, you heard right, they were into communication. Can you hear the powers of fate going 'Ha ha, Lucy'? There was Lucy, who can't actually talk to men, stuck in a moving vehicle with some fellas who were well into talking about feelings. Like these boys were so into talking about feelings that they'd made it a proper scheduled activity, like watching *Enders*, or sorting out the recycling. They would 'check in' and ask each other how they were feeling. Yep, terrifying or what?

And when they were 'checking in' they were liable to close their eyes and talk about their feelings for about twelve minutes. No handy little, 'Fine thanks, you?' from these guys. When one had finished, the other would start. It was based on some personal development work that the Light-Haired German had recently partaken in.

Now this, for me, was about as comfortable and easy as inserting a cauliflower up my rectum. But I did rather enjoy witnessing the boys do it. Wow. And blimey, there was something amazing about having access to someone's thoughts, feelings and sensations in this way. So often we guess how someone is feeling, and assume we know. But we don't, we can't. 'Oh, so and so's pissed off with me,' we think, not knowing that earlier that day so and so saw her ex-boyfriend kissing another girl and she's really just trying to get through the day without sobbing. Light-Haired German was so sensitive, and being allowed to witness his inner world and all its vulnerability felt really special. I literally felt a surge of warmth in my chest towards him.

I should probably casually mention here that I thought the Dark-Haired German was frickin' BEAUTIFUL. He was tall, dark and handsome, with a lovely smile, and really, trust me on this, quite amazing eyes. The eyes of a wildcat. A panther. Yes, his eyes were so amazing they made me come up with dreadful similes about them. He looked almost uncannily like my first love, which was simultaneously comforting and really freaky. I also thought him wise, like Buddha in the Bedroom Next Door but with a cute German accent.

The Dark-Haired German did one of these check-in things the day after we met. I watched him, thinking, 'He's just divine,' and trying to close my mouth. Then he suddenly turned to me. 'It is nice to meet you,' he started, but then he screwed his face up as though it had just come into close proximity with a very well-established case of athlete's foot, voiced a low guttural moaning sound as though he'd just backed his car into the garage door, shook his head, and said, looking terrified, 'But you're so fast. You're like a volcano. I don't know how I feel about you. Sometimes I want to run away.'

Whoa, not finding this communication thing quite so wowzers now. I wanted to cry. I really, really wanted to cry.

Afterwards this heavy 'I'm about to cry' feeling stayed with me. I sat in the back of the car, spookily quiet for me. I'd been so happy recently and getting so much better at the self-loving thing, I didn't want this comment to bring me down, but I could feel it powerfully trying to do so. I wished I'd been able to laugh it off, or say to him, 'Wow, so you find me a bit much, tell me more,' but I didn't. I let it silence me. I thought I was learning to love myself, but if I really, really loved myself then that comment wouldn't hurt me. It wouldn't have mattered what anyone said about me.

My best girlfriend often says, 'Slow down and say that all again,' when I'm speaking. (I spend a lot of time on my own, writing, you see, so quite often I explode with excitement when I get to talk to real people.) English is her first language and even she can't understand me when I vomit a volley of words at her. I know I'm fast. And I don't feel like crying when my best mate tells me so.

Ah ha, but the Dark-Haired German was a man. Maybe I could take hearing a judgement from a woman, but not from a man. I definitely couldn't take hearing a judgement from this man, because I felt flickers of emotional tears behind my eyes for about three hours after. Three hours after!!! I was thirty-five. Even a four-year-old would have recovered after ten minutes and got back to giggling about the word 'poo'.

Why couldn't I hear any type of criticism from a man? Why? Uh oh, you know what's coming. I had a theory, and this one made me quite cross.

Actually, it made me so angry that I wanted a rebate from the Exchequer for all the tax I'd ever paid because I couldn't help but feel that society had royally ballsed up my ability to be a sane person when it came to dealing with men.

I believe that I got upset when the beautiful Dark-Haired German criticised me because I'd been bloomin' well conditioned by our society to always behave in a way that will please men and therefore it feels dreadful, as though I have failed in the most spectacular way, when I don't. Our society gives the power to the men and has the women running around trying to get positive responses from them. We wouldn't wear Wonderbras or get Brazilians if this wasn't the case. Teenage girls wouldn't be wearing agonising lap-dancer shoes and giving unreciprocated blowjobs in nightclub toilets, among many other things, if this wasn't the case. We wouldn't have all read a gazillion 'How to Make Him Fall in Love with You' and 'How to Make Him

Notice You Tonight' articles if this wasn't the case. I wouldn't be snogging men I didn't want to for fear of not pleasing them if this wasn't the case.

Anyway. I'd wanted communication, and I'd got it. It was hard, but in the end I was glad, as it had got me thinking. (And I still thought he was a beautiful man.)

It's not so much about how my body looks as how it FEELS!!

So there I was on this road trip with two Germans and I was a bit confused. I couldn't work out if they were completely bonkers or totally sorted. It wasn't just the communication games. There was more. More. *Mehr!* They did something else that was weird – and this was proper weird, like 'peanut butter with jam' weird, or 'a train to Reading costing more than a flight to Venice' weird. The Germans frequently asked each other a question that I'd never heard before. Ever. Well, except maybe at the doctor's. And it was this: 'How are you feeling in your body?' Yep. 'How are you feeling in your body?' I couldn't work out whether it was weird that they did this, or weird that no one else did it. Because actually . . . it was quite fun. Well, it *became* fun. At first it wasn't fun. At all.

The first time I heard this question I was sitting in the back of the car, trying not to cry because the Dark-Haired German had just told me that I terrified him. I was wondering whether I should get an early flight home, thus removing my volcanic self from the Dark-Haired German's presence so he could enjoy his holiday. I noticed the Dark-Haired German looking at me through the rear-view mirror. I caught his eye. Uh oh. The Dark-Haired German's eyes. Now we have to pop down a bridle path to discuss his BEAUTIFUL eyes again. His greeny hazel eyes with brown freckly bits in them. (I'd recently written a novel where the main man, Joe King, had greeny hazel eyes with brown freckly bits in. I had an extreme crush on the fictional Joe King . . . I think I might have been doing some single woman fantasising when I wrote him.)

'How do you feel in your body?' the Dark-Haired German asked me.

I averted my gaze from these PHENOMENAL eyes and mumbled the only obvious and sensible English answer: 'Um, fine.'

And I carried on looking out of the window, while the Germans asked each other the same question. And, BLIMEY, they had all sorts of crazy shit going on in their bodies, swirly heat and energy and colours and all sorts. Curious, I had a quick internal inspection myself. Maybe I had got some crazy-ass lava-lamp-funk stuff going on in me too. Sadly not. I was less lamp, more lump. I felt heavy and sludgy, like a massive dark ugly slug was crawling through my veins. My forehead was flickering like I wanted to cry. And since I'd recently looked into the Dark-Haired German's eyes, it felt as though there was a tiny fairy gymnast in my tummy. And the tiny fairy gymnast was really into twiddling. But I liked it. Not the feeling like arse bit. The seeing how I was feeling in my body bit. Because there was so much happening.

I realised that throughout my life I'd spent a lot of time worrying and thinking about how my body looked, but not how it *felt*.

So, yes, I got well into the 'how do you feel in your body?' question. Asking it, answering it, I was all over it. Actually, I was quite into just sitting there and feeling what was happening in my body. I love a good distraction, and this one was free. But there were so many sensations in my body that I'd never really paid any attention to.

When I watched the Germans together and saw how well they got on and how much they loved each other, I got this warm feeling in my chest, I really did. And when I went for a walk and accidentally ended up clambering over a rocky ravine and I looked down, I felt my throat and chest constrict in fear, and something definitely occurring in my bowels.

Although when the Dark-Haired German asked me how I was feeling in my body, I had to lie. Because some serious internal stuff happened to me when the Dark-Haired German was around. We had bonded in Spain, over Dalí, Gaudí and those very small bottles of cava, so I didn't feel that I terrified the poor man so much any more. But if he knew what occurred in certain areas when he was near me, he would be under the table, cowering and calling the emergency services.

It wasn't just his eyes or his smile or that his touch felt like magic, or the fact that he'd drive off route saying, 'I read that there's a picturesque village here. I thought we could visit' (oh, I love a picturesque village, me), or the fact that he'd learned tantra, and he talked openly about sex in what I felt was a very beautiful way. I had told him all about my attempts at embarking on a sexual odyssey, all I had learned, and all I wanted to experience. He listened and nodded as though it was the most natural thing in the world when I told him that what I really wanted to experience was very, very slow sex. And he pronounced vagina like 'vag(rhymes with bag)-eena' and . . . and . . . oh, someone turn me off at the mains, I need to cool down.

SERIOUS ENERGY gallivanted around my body whenever the Dark-Haired German was near me. It was so serious it could enter *Mastermind* with a chosen subject of the Franco-Prussian War. And it was proper powerful. I was creating so much energy I felt I could probably have lighted and heated all of Wales. And I suppose it would be powerful if you consider that the feeling I got when I was near the Dark-Haired German was actually the start of all life, because we, humans, generally start out with a feeling of swirly, glorious sex energy. Followed by a bonk.

But I knew that bonking the Dark-Haired German was out of the question. And oddly enough, that was OK. In the past when I'd had crushes I'd been desperate for the other person to reciprocate, perhaps because the rejection would have been too much to bear. But this time, well, I didn't feel like that. I wasn't sitting there willing him to want me. I could just admire this man and feel attracted to him. Maybe finding out early on that he found me challenging had stopped me getting my hopes up. Or maybe I was enjoying all the glorious sensations that being attracted to a beautiful man created in my body. Whatever it was, I was grateful, because I felt alive, and sexual, and womanly, heavenly and a little bit giddy. And perhaps best of all, I suspected that I was growing out of being such a mentalist with the opposite sex. Hurrah! I was in the throes of a big, all right, MASSIVE crush. And it was all rather divine.

An erection on the beach

Then one day in Mallorca I was walking to the beach. Well, it was less a beach, more a very rocky secluded cove. I'd been swimming at the rocky secluded cove because I didn't have a bikini. Well, technically I did have a bikini, but when I put it on the elastic just couldn't be bothered to be elastic and the knickers went all Tarzan flappy pants. So I had taken to wearing my dark underwear and swimming in the rocky secluded cove.

I didn't swim with the Germans, because they were German and I figured they probably swam naked. I'd already bumped into the Light-Haired German as he strolled up the stairs of our villa with nothing on. At all. Willy out. Balls. Everything. As though it was normal. I did what any courageous leader of her own personal sexual revolution would do. I stopped breathing, looked the other way, and ran into my room to recover. I'm not just English. I also went to a convent, remember. Buggered. Where was I? Oh, yes. The beach.

So it was really hot. I don't know what the clouds were up to but they were not in the sky. The beach was empty except for two people. A fisherman. And . . . the object of my (MASSIVE) crush. The Dark-Haired German.

He was sitting on a rock, writing in a notebook. I wrote in notebooks too. We were made for each other. He looked up and smiled. He had a Peter Pan smile. The Dark-Haired German was stubbly and manly, but he smiled like a delighted boy.

'Are you going to swim?' he asked.

'Um . . .' I replied. I know. I'm brilliant. This was a bit of an 'oh, cocks' situation. You see, I couldn't strip down to my pants in front of the Dark-Haired German. I mean, I know I'd been working on loving myself. But it was one thing saying I loved my bum in a mirror and quite another getting said bum out in the presence of a beautiful man.

'Let's swim,' he said, standing up.

'Errrr,' I replied. He started to unbutton his shirt.

'I don't have a swimming costume,' I whispered.

'Neither do I,' he said. Wowzers, I thought, and I pulled my dress over my head.

I stood on the pebbles in just my underwear. He started to take his trousers off. I looked the other way. Out at the diamanté sea.

'Ah, oh,' he started. 'Hmmm.'

This was unusual. It was normally me with the vocabulary of a Teletubby.

'I, er, ahhh. I have an erection. I thought I should bring attention to it, so I don't feel so embarrassed.'

Blimey, there was a courgette camping in his boxer shorts. Which perhaps I shouldn't have been staring at. I looked away. But caught his eye. I smiled, politely. The convent taught me to be polite. Sadly, the convent didn't teach me what to do or what to think when the man you fancy, but are convinced doesn't like you, gets a mightily exciting erection on the beach. I opted for the failsafe 'carry on as though nothing's happened' approach and we walked into the water and swam.

Later, we headed back to the villa. I walked beside him in the sun. I felt a bit – quite a fair bit – aroused. My skin had been slapped alive by the cool water. A warm breeze was dancing about my body. All my sexy places were tingling. My nipples were erect. The Dark-Haired German was at my side. I could barely breathe.

'How do you feel in your body?' he asked.

'Oh. Oh. Oh. Amazing,' I smiled. Well, I could hardly say I was practically having an orgasm, could I? 'What about you?'

'This whole side of my body that's near you is hot, like it's on fire,' he said.

We carried on walking. But I didn't say anything else. I couldn't. I felt shy, as though I was about thirteen.

Much later on, we were outside looking at the stars. He moved his seat close to mine and placed his hand on my back. I could hear my heart beating. He looked into my eyes.

'What do you want to do?' he asked me.

'All I want to do is kiss you,' I whispered, and I leaned forward and slowly touched his lips with mine.

That's not what really happened, is it, Lucy? Well, not exactly. No. But one day, one day very soon, I would be that woman. I would!

So, Lucy, what was it you actually said when he asked you what you wanted to do?

I said, 'I don't know,' and went to bed. Alone. Where I twirled around and around in my duvet, my thoughts going something like this:

'LUCY! LUCY! You total twatting plum! Communication! Communication!

'You've been thinking on and on and wanking well on about communication. Your entire history with men has been marked by you not communicating what you feel. Then, when you get the opportunity to tell the bloke you fancy how you feel, you come up with, "hmmm, amazing" and "I don't know". I don't feckin' know!!!!! I don't feckin' wanking sodding know!!!!!!'

But then suddenly, I stopped. I extricated myself from the Duvet Twizzler I'd got myself into, left my bed and tiptoed upstairs to the Dark-Haired German's room. His door was open. He was sleeping. But he woke. I knelt down by his bed, speaking quickly.

'Hello, sorry to wake you. I just want to say two things to you. When you asked me earlier how I was feeling in my body, well, I was on fire for you, I was, like . . .' Communication, Lucy, do it, do it DOOOO ITTTTT. 'I was aroused. And then when you said what do you want to do? All I wanted to do was kiss you. Every fibre in my body wanted to kiss you. Um, yes, so I just wanted to tell you that. Now go back to sleep.'

And with that I Usain Bolted it out of there and got back into bed. A minute later there was a knock on my door.

An unfortunate handjob

I FOUND MYSELF IN AN ADULT-FUN-NAKEDNESS SITUATION WITH A BLOKE WHO KNEW ABOUT MY MISSION!!! High five. I thank you. And this was unlike anything I'd experienced. I was actually communicating, for a start (to be fair, this wasn't so much of my own volition, more part of the daily holiday routine) and I was pretty much sober (having consumed just a civilised glass of red wine, and not a single Jägerbomb or pint of Stella).

But – there was a but – one teeny weensy ickle little but. I had started to go all batshit crazy. You know all those things I had been working hard to overcome, the self-flagellation and all the rest? Well, on me getting it on with said fella, they got really inflamed and swelled to an elephantine size.

This metamorphosis wasn't in effect all the time. Thank the twinkly stars. No, I wasn't a cockwomble all the time, just quite a lot of the time. And the thing that could be absolutely, definitely 'put your house down on that bad boy, it's a dead cert' relied upon was that my self-saboteur would pop up at *the* most inopportune times imaginable. Seriously, the timing was so dreadful I was almost impressed by it.

Yes, it struck at spectacularly prime-time moments. Like my first foray into penis territory. When I was giving him a little handjob.

I was in bed with the Dark-Haired German. We were naked. I do like that fact. I'll repeat it. I was there, naked, and he was there, naked. And there was this big erect penis between us. He'd just touched me in all manner of gentle, slow, delicious, tender ways, and now I wanted to reciprocate. I wanted to give him the swirly sensations of surrender he'd just given me, to render him all gooey like a washed-up jellyfish, as he had me.

So, I started to touch this masterpiece of a big erect penis, but then I suddenly remembered that I didn't know what I was supposed to do with it. It had been a while since I last hung out with a penis, and that time I was drunk and holding a manual. And that hadn't ended well. I froze. It all went a bit 'GAAAHHHHHHHH' in my head. Maybe I had developed an actual proper phobia. I panicked. I'd never met this particular penis before. It looked to be a very nice penis. I liked it and I wanted it to like me it too. It's just I wasn't really sure how to make that happen.

To give myself credit, I had a rough idea of what to do with a willy. But I wasn't feeling confident enough – or drunk enough – to put it all into practice. I know that when boys wank they yank, and there was a fair bit of yanking in online porn too. But I'd only just met this willy and yanking it just seemed wrong. With yanking out, I did a bit of stroking instead. But my confidence was plummeting. And my old self-saboteur loves it when my confidence starts to wane, so it jumped at this opportunity to assuredly inform me that I was the worst lover in the world and that I would never be able to satisfy this man like he satisfied me.

I carried on stroking and did a bit of yanking too. But a right racket was going on in my mind.

'LUCY, THIS IS THE WORST HANDJOB IN THE HISTORY OF HANDJOBS! LIKE, SERIOUSLY, SOMEONE WILL PROBABLY STORM THROUGH THE DOOR AND GIVE YOU A TROPHY IN A MOMENT.' On and on she went. And on.

And then after a while I laughed. A little 'oh Lucy, oh self-saboteur, you are such an arse' laugh. Only it seemed that he was about to ejaculate. And I'd just laughed. Yep. Awkward. Afterwards, he said, 'Why did you laugh before my ejaculation?' (He pronounced it e-yack-ulation – very cute.)

'Don't tell him,' my self-saboteur whispered. 'He'll think you're a total spanner. Tell him it was a little cough.'

Instead, I decided, rather radically, to tell the truth. 'I got all paranoid that I wasn't able to satisfy you. I think you're a really beautiful lover,' I explained. 'I think it was a nervous laugh. A laugh at my own rubbishness. I'm sorry. It can't have been nice.'

He did look at me as though I was odd. But I felt much better. We carried on fiddling with and smiling at each other. Luckily, all was well for the time being. Only blimey, it was all a bit concerning and stressful because this self-saboteur was powerful. I had thought I'd got the old Twat Self under control in normal life but it was in OVERDRIVE now there was a man on the scene. And I was scared, worried it could smash this glorious thing that was happening with the Dark-Haired German.

And the thing that saddened me the most was that all my insecure, self-sabotaging thoughts stole me away from the amazing moments that I was having. Take the handjob scenario: what a brilliant moment in time that was. I was on a Mediterranean island, I'd just had an orgasm, and was exploring a beautiful man's naked body. Why couldn't I just have been in that moment? Why couldn't I just have been there, feeling his heat, feeling all the different textures of his skin, feeling how he responded to my touch, feeling my own responses to his body, how my breathing quickened, how my instincts wanted to touch him there or there?

Why wasn't I simply feeling and experiencing all that awesomeness? Why did I have to massively overcomplicate things with thoughts of porn-star yanking and how crap I was?

Slow sex

The slow sex, when we finally had it, was bloomin' amazing.

How slow did we go? Oh, reeeeeeally slow. Sting would have been proud. We did the looking into each other's eyes for ages and everything. You know those times where you set off a bit fast, you aren't connected, and you clunk teeth or nut each other? Well, there wasn't a sniff of that. Hurrah! Normally I or the chap would have felt one of us should be doing *something* and speeded it up with a kiss, a grope, or whatever the next stage of the 'normal, slightly porny sex' was. But here, we were actively and deliberately going *really* slowly.

This meant that there was a fair amount of doing bugger all except breathing. But blimey, breathing had never been so awesome. Deep breaths, quivery breaths, breaths you felt on your neck that tingled your pussy.

(I need to take you aside for a moment. That is the first time I've written 'pussy', and I'm not sure I'm feeling it. I tried the slang dictionary for vagina, and the first line offered me 'axe wound, badly wrapped kebab, bang hole, bat cave, bean, bearded clam'. You think that's depressing, you should see the rest. Huge deviation here, I know, but it will become more important in the next chapters. I actually like the word 'cunt' – as a word it sounds strong enough to birth a small human, epic, capable of magic and adventure, and also somehow all-knowing and final: you wouldn't want to mess with a cunt.)

Where was I? Oh yes, HAVING STUPENDOUSLY SLOW SEX. So first of all, let's talk about the build-up to the first kiss! It was like a billion *X Factor* results announcements, all that tension and excitement, 'When will it happen – we're frigging waiting!!' There was a lot of the badass breathing going on, holding our mouths close together, smiling, playing with each other. Then when our lips did meet, mouths have never been so exciting, so wet and warm, oh, and so great for nibbling, licking and nipping.

Sometimes the not touching was as arousing or more arousing than the actual touching. A hand not quite touching my breast, just hovering there, as my vagina contracted. Or my hand, or mouth, near but not quite making contact with his hard penis.

I was reeeally turned on. I think I might have orgasmed before he even made contact with my vulva. And yet, in starting so slowly I was able to have sex that was harder and faster than I had ever found comfortable before. In fact, blimey, I have to say that, I, Lucy, revved up to become a bit of a wild explosive guttural-sounding sex beast. It was good to meet her but, jeez, the sounds! The noises I was making – I'd never heard anything like it – it was as though they were coming from a woman who'd been trapped in a cave for 2,000 years. Now, I realise that seems odd but these sounds that came out of me felt, well the only word I can think of to describe them is 'ancient'. They definitely weren't porn noises. More like howls of pain from a long, long time ago.

So this, my friends, brings us back to the slow sex prologue. And after that first time you'd assume that I'd jump up afterwards and start singing 'ai ai yippee', wouldn't you? Well, I didn't. I cried. I lay there naked and I wept. I am so not cool.

'Why are you crying?' he asked.

'I didn't think I deserved to be touched like that,' I said.

He kissed me and that phrase, 'I didn't think I deserved to be touched like that', kept repeating in my mind. I think I was crying for all the sex I'd had before that was rough, disconnected, or desensitised by alcohol. Somehow, being touched tenderly brought up the sadness of all the times I had not been touched lovingly there.

The crying felt good, though, healing even, and I let it happen while he held me.

Previously, I'd had this longing for slow sex, but I don't think I'd fully understood why. Yes, I had found sex to be too quick, all a bit hands here, legs there, mouth here, penis in . . . aaaand done. What slowing down the whole process did for me was that it actually connected me to it.

But after this whole journey I'd been on I felt much more connected to, um, everything, I think. I felt more connected to myself sexually, because I'd thought about what I wanted to experience and not experience in the realm of sex. I was no longer flailing around, simply taking what was going.

But I was also more connected to the person I was. I recognised that I had a habit of being a bit weak when it came to men, of finding it hard to speak up. Having previously been cruel to myself, I was now trying to be kinder. I had more understanding and awareness of who I was than ever before.

Also, of course, I was having sober sex, and as I've said before, this was a big deal. The sex felt amazing, because I could *feel* it. In the same way I've cut my leg when drunk and not even realised until the next day, the analgesic effects of booze had denied me the pleasure I was seeking.

Also, and this is a biggie too, I was more connected to the physical experience I was having. I wasn't in my head telling myself I was a fat twat, I was in my body feeling sublime. I had been enjoying all the sensations in my body just from being around the Dark-Haired German for days. I was experiencing my body in a way I never had before. I realised I'd spent so much time in the chatter of my head I'd been completely missing out on what was going in the rest of me. And when I took this new awareness to sex it was fan-frigging – how long is this orgasm going on for? – tastic.

Also, sorry, there's more, I was more connected to the fella because I'd been nothing but honest with him. It wasn't like the internet dating with the half-true profile; this guy had grasped what I was looking for because I'd spoken openly about it: he knew I wanted to explore slow sex and a host of other things. He understood I'd been on a bit of a vertiginous learning curve. For the first time in my life I was chatting away openly to a man about my sexual needs, and also about my personal journey.

In many ways I don't think I'd ever been this 'me' before.

Now, some people might be reading this and thinking,

'Oh, she was just in love.' Sex is amazing when you're in love, especially at the start. And yes, I did feel a lot of 'love' for this man, but I didn't want to marry him, and I was able to let him go when the time came. It wasn't like any 'love' I'd ever experienced before.

Everything felt different, and that was because I was different. And one thing I was sure of was that this looking-at-my-sexuality malarkey was the best thing I had ever done.

ORGASMS, PLEASURE AND POWER

Lucy's old masturbatory habits

Dark-Haired German and I carried on our relationship after the holiday, and one consequence of having a lover in another country was that it got me masturbating.

But my masturbatory habits completely changed. Incidents of self-pleasure had historically looked something like this:

Time
Afternoon or evening. Nothing against the morning, but I barely left myself enough time to shower before leaving the house let alone to lie about having a climactic fiddle.

Place
My unmade bed.

Outfit
Whatever garb I had on when the urge to wank took hold.

Accessories
That old romantic combo of human and laptop in bed. I'm surprised there aren't more pop songs or poems about it.

What normally happened

Something would activate me beforehand, perhaps a flirtation, an attraction, reading or seeing something particularly sexy in life, print or on the telly, or just sexy imaginings that I couldn't get out of my head. I would feel stirred up and take myself off to my room for some 'me time'. Then I'd sit and search for some porn I liked the look of. I tended to go for 'lesbian' porn, straight porn where there was a fair bit of foreplay or female-friendly threesomes. It would arouse me seeing a woman having her breasts and nipples stimulated.

Once I found something I liked I would come pretty quickly. I wouldn't undress or play with myself as such, although I might push my crotch against the denim of my jeans, say, or press my hand down towards my clitoris. My orgasm would last a few seconds and that would be it. If I was drunk I could spend longer looking at various bits of porn. Afterwards I'd always delete my computer's history and get on with other stuff.

Porn in a nutshell

Now, I'm assuming you spend your time furtively rubbing your bits in front of the computer like me. But in case you don't . . . For those of you not acquainted with online porn, here it is, in a nutshell, or rather a HELLUVA LOTTA NUTS.

Online porn is pretty much dominated by some big free sites which until recently were all owned by the same person: a German chap called Fabian.[1]

There is LOADS of sex on these sites. Minutes and minutes, hours and hours, YEARS worth of rutting. And Fabian very kindly categorised all these how's your fathers for us. Bless him, otherwise we'd be all over the shop. Fabian offers us many, many flavours of sexual congress, including Teen, Lesbian, Anal, MILF,

Orgy, Creampie, Facial, Shemale. Ebony, Big Butt, Blowjobs . . .
you get the idea.

A few points I should mention

Creampie – doesn't involve cake (semen and orifices).
Facial – has nothing to do with skincare (semen and faces).
MILF – in case you don't know, is Mothers I'd Like to Fuck.
Teen – On these sites it means over eighteen, although quite often
it will be implied that the women are younger, say by wearing a
school uniform, cheerleader outfit or more childish underwear
and pulled-up socks.

The general set-up is this

You enter a site and see a screen that lists all these different categories
and many more. There are little pictures delineating each.

'Ooo, which genre am I feeling today?' you might muse as
you look at the screen. 'Perhaps a bit of creampie . . . or maybe
a gangbang. Decisions, decisions . . .' You decide what you fancy,
and click on creampie, say, which will likely be annotated by an
image of a woman's anus or vagina with semen visible in it. Once
you've clicked you are again faced with a screen of pictures to
choose from. These are the videos on offer, page after page after
page . . . and on and on. If you decided now that for the rest of
your life you wanted to watch online porn without stopping, you
wouldn't get through it. Blimey, I doubt you'd even get through the
whole creampie section. Man, there's a LOT of sex on the internet.

There are little tags to help you streamline your search, which
tend to categorise the women yet further – i.e. redhead, puffy
nipples – and what goes on, i.e. blowjob, first-time anal. The
videos range in duration from a few minutes to half an hour
and generally will be a taster type thing from another site, which
wants you to subscribe and pay money to see more content.

A few more points to note

There is loads of semen in online porn
Oh my goodness, yes, you should probably pack a mac.

In pornography, the shot where the male ejaculates is known as the money shot. I've no idea where the term came from or what it really means. A big old capitalist orgasm? I find it interesting that the king of shots is always the male orgasm. As though the female orgasm doesn't count. The prize is the money shot, the male orgasm. Now, I'm a big fan of female orgasms myself, and there are so many different types of them. What about the fourteen variations of female orgasm? Where are the two-minute shots of a man staring wide-eyed in wonder as a woman climaxes? Well, to be fair, they probably are there somewhere, but they definitely do not constitute the norm.

There are billions of blowjobs in online porn
And I'm not even exaggerating. Porn is crammed to the rafters full of blowjobs, the majority of which follow a similar pattern: woman (or women) on her (their) knees, man looming over her (them), her eyes open, looking up at him while the man holds the woman's head down. The hand on the head thing pretty much always happens in porn. Now, call me old-fashioned, but if I'm giving a man's penis pleasure with my mouth, if I'm bestowing what is essentially a bit of a gift, I at least want to be able to come up for air should I need to.

And bloomin' *tonnes* of anal sex
Honestly, seriously, if you haven't seen porn I'm worried you won't be able to imagine a virtual place with so many stretched sphincters.

Kissing is very rare in online porn

Whereas pretty much 99 per cent (I am totally guessing here) of the sex that most people have starts with kissing, most of the sex you'll see online won't involve kissing at all. There is some, though, and I always find it a little unusual or startling.

There's not really much touching or caressing in online porn either

Lesbian porn is hugely popular in online porn

It generally doesn't feature lesbians, though it does tend to include women kissing and a bit of caressing.

Women are pretty much never called women in online porn

They tend to be referred to as sluts. Also, girls, babes, bitches, whores, hoes.

Often the premise of the porn clips is women being duped

For example, women going to a casting for a modelling job and then being asked/persuaded to strip, give a blowjob, have sex with two men. Or a taxi driver who promises he won't share the video or put it on the internet as he coerces a woman to have sex with him.

And don't forget the ads! (Actually you won't very well be able to forget the ads as they will be flashing repeatedly and popping up all over your online experience . . . not to mention the gambling websites that will just open themselves in new browsers on your screen.)

Yes, sirreee, most of these sites have adverts too; these tend to be for National Trust family days out and Maltesers. Not really!! The ads on big free porn sites fall into two main categories: 'HOW TO GET A PROPOSTEROUSLY LONG PENIS!!!!' and

'These sluts want to have SEX with YOU now and they are next door to you and they are sooooooo desperate for YOU!!' The penis adverts will feature a man standing naked and looming over his long penis. The sex ones will feature pictures of women that flash up one after another and they will keep telling you how they are filthy sluts who are desperate to fuck you. Me??! Lucy in Sussex . . . really? Golly.

And for now, that is an overview of the big free porn sites; I hope you're still with me. Let's press on!

How many types of orgasm am I capable of?

So my masturbatory habits had historically followed a predictable, and somewhat lacklustre, pattern. But I was struck by this rumour I'd heard that women were capable of fourteen different types of orgasm. If this was true then I was majorly missing my target by having these quickly snatched clitoral ones.

I did a bit of research to find out what these orgasms entailed, and what I discovered I found to be . . . well, fascinating and infuriating and heartbreaking and oddly life-changing too.

First of all, I took to Google to find out if there was any truth in the fourteen figure and wow, articles on Google confirmed that I, Lucy-Anne Holmes, person with a pussy, was a PLEASURE MACHINE!!! Yes, I was capable of fourteen types of orgasm, oh hang about, no, other articles I read told me it was three types of orgasm, seven types of orgasm, nine types of orgasm, four types of orgasm, twelve types of orgasm! Hmmm. Articles on Google told me a lot of stuff, but it didn't always agree with itself. I'd heard of the G-spot orgasm, although I wasn't entirely sure where mine was or if we'd ever met. I found out it was named G-spot after the fella who 'discovered' it, Ernst Gräfenberg. I might call mine Ernst. Although, hold up, some articles I read said there was no such thing as a G-spot at all. Riiiight.

I found myself leaping about Google and scouring books, more and more curious about the subject of female anatomy and pleasure. I was a woman in her thirties discovering this information for herself, and yet at the same time I had this feeling that I was uncovering and unearthing facts that weren't widely known to the majority of women. I was digging all this treasure up and thinking, 'What the hell are you doing way down here in the first place? You should be polished and out on the mantelpiece.'

For a start, I realised that I didn't even know my own pleasure map. I would look at diagrams of the genitalia I owned and exclaim, 'Oh so *that's* what that bit is called!' or, 'Oops, I've had *that* wrong my whole life.' For example, I had never really been sure what my vulva was. I knew it was a bit 'down there', but no more than that. It emerged that I had been saying 'vagina' when I hadn't actually been referring to my vagina at all. I finally got wind of the facts: the vagina is the inside tubey bit and the vulva (pretty word, potentially useful for naming daughters?) is all the outside stuff – your undercarriage, if you like. Rather excitingly, the only word that means the inner and outer bits is that gloriously pithy word, 'cunt'. Cunt. Ooo, I know I've said it before, but what a word. What an area. I had by now developed a fondness for pronouncing it perfectly and delivering it with a smile. (Although don't whatever you do refer to unscrupulous politicians and people you don't like as cunts; as stand-up comedian Kate Smurthwaite says, it's an insult to cunts.)*

Also, and this one was weird, despite having been a lifelong pee-er I had never really been sure where this pee actually came from. It always felt as though I peed from my vagina; occasionally

---

* This quote is from her stand-up show. She also adds, 'I've got one and not only is it brilliant, despite my best efforts it hasn't closed down any hospitals.'

I wondered whether I was dodgily plumbed and no one had noticed. Turns out my urethra (the hole that the pee comes out of) is located just inside my vagina, hence the confusion. We're all a bit different down there, so it might not feel the same for everyone. I like to think of us all being unique down there, like our own intimate fingerprint.

Vag lips is what I used to call the labia, another pretty word, sounds like an aristocrat's daughter. Labia have gorgeous shapes; some lips hang down and look, I think, like a flower. I started to think how beautiful the vulva was, but with nicknames for this area like 'axe wound', I wasn't surprised that generally us women aren't proud of our bits.

And I realised that I'd had the clitoris all wrong. I thought it was a little bean. But actually the bit of the clitoris you can see is just a small part of it; there is much more behind the scenes. In 2005, it was discovered that internally it is actually a wishbone shape. The clitoral glans is the little bean bit that looks like it's just a quarter to a half inch long, but in fact extends backwards into two branches called 'crura' that are each about three to three and a half inches in length.[2]

Yes, that's right: in 2005 it was discovered that there was more to the clitoris than meets the eye.[3] Strange, do you not think, that it took until 2005 for this to become known, when as far as I am aware, the female body has been around for thousands of years? I delved further, and found out that in 1948, the twenty-fifth edition of *Gray's Anatomy*, the authority on the human body, came out, and in it there was absolutely NO MENTION OF THE CLITORIS. Yes, a bit of the body that had existed in the previous editions (just labelled on a diagram, mind, not actually elaborated upon) DISAPPEARED.[4] How could the clitoris have disappeared from a medical manual in the twentieth century? How could we only have realised how big it was in 2005? Something strange was going on with the clitoris.

I also learned that it is MEGA SENSITIVE, with two to three times more nerve endings than the penis. Wow. We have LOADS more nerve endings than the boys. Why aren't clitorises running the world?! And it is the only bit on a male or female body that is there solely for pleasure.[5] Yee-haw. Let the good times roll. And it belongs to the girls. Hi fives, sisters.

And yet, as I sat and thought about it and researched it, I saw that life had been an absolute bastard to this little twinkle, this hotspot of female sexuality. Throughout history and across the world the clitoris has been ignored, lambasted or actually cut off. And that is a really fucking sobering thought. The only bit of the human body that is solely for pleasure resides on the female of the species and it is *cut from us*. On what planet could this happen? Oh – ours.

A little history of the clitoris

Going way back, the Greeks and Romans believed the clitoris (and remember that for millennia, the clitoris was thought to be just the glans, 'little hill' – the meaning of *kleitoris*, its root word in Greek) to be a bit of a crap attempt at a penis.[6] They thought that women were lesser, or deformed, versions of men. Thanks, guys. Ancient Greek physician Claudius Galen argued that as the more perfect sex, men had sufficient body heat to allow genital protrusion, while weaker women's genitalia remained hidden from view.

Ancient texts also confirm the practice of female genital cutting, although from what I gather it's a little hazy as to where and when it originated. Apparently, there is evidence from Herodotus that by around 500 BCE the Egyptians, Phoenicians, Hittites and Ethiopians were all practising female cutting. There are also differing reasons for doing it across different societies. It could have been to keep girls and women 'pure', physically and morally; in Sudan and Egypt, the Arabic word *tahur* – purification – is used to describe the actual procedure. It is also speculated that it might have served to 'establish unambiguous gender identity' like that of the gods.[7]

Jumping now to fifteenth-century Europe, in 1486 *The Malleus Maleficarum*, otherwise known as *The Hammer of Witches*, is published. It is written by a couple of Catholic clergymen, and it is basically the definitive guide to finding, torturing and killing witches, who were predominantly women. It calls the aroused and engorged clitoris 'the devil's teat', and says it's evidence of dealings with the devil, or witchcraft. This treatise isn't just a little mini micro blip in humanity: it is followed for OVER TWO CENTURIES.[8]

In 1545, a fella called Charles Estienne does the first dissection of the clitoris. The findings he publishes in his book about the human body are inaccurate and he refers to the clitoris as the woman's 'shameful member'.[9] Oh, do bog off, Charles.

But good news is coming, in Italy at least. In 1559 Renaldus Columbus 'discovers' the clit![10] Although he prefers to call it 'the love or sweetness of Venus'. Bless him! He says that it is 'pre-eminently the seat of women's delight'. Whadda guy! And things continue to look perkier for the clitoris over the next few centuries in Europe, with various medical men and even a woman, a midwife, making reference to it and its ability to make women 'lustful' and enjoy a bit of the old nooky.[11] Although, it's no cause for a party because in Europe and the USA in the nineteenth-century doctors were removing clitorises as a cure for masturbation and insanity.

Then in the twentieth century Freud stomps in with some bonkers theory that everyone goes wild about. Yes, world-renowned Austrian neurologist Sigmund Freud introduced a theory that clitoral orgasms were immature and vaginal orgasms mature. WHA? He thought that the clitoris was just for pre-pubescent orgasms but after puberty, 'with the change to femininity the clitoris should wholly or in part hand over its sensitivity, and at the same time its importance, to the vagina'.[12] Weird, eh.

Then in 1948, the twenty-fifth edition of *Gray's Anatomy* forgets to mention the clitoris at all.

In the West, the remainder of the century sees studies 'unearthing' the pleasure potential of the clitoris. Even as I was growing up in Britain in the eighties I remember there being a sense that the clitoris was somehow newly discovered, I seem to remember many jokes about men not being able to find it. Then, in 2005, Dr Helen O'Connell discovers that it is way more than just the little chickpea people had hitherto thought.

And yet female genital mutilation is still going on today. Statistics estimate that 200 million women and girls alive today in thirty countries (predominantly across Africa and Asia) have been cut.[13] And there we have the tragic story of the clitoris. Can we please give it a happy ending? Can we please create a world where all clitorises are free, and where each woman can choose what happens to this part of her body?

I had set off all wanky clappedy, all 'heigh ho, let's have a fiddle!' and before I knew it I had fallen down a hole, staring gobsmacked at a world that expects half the population to be beautiful and subservient, and even physically cuts their capacity for pleasure from them. And yet I wasn't in a strange land, I was simply in our world, looking at it with fresh eyes.

Turning my attention to the G-spot, I found out that it was located a little way up my vagina on the belly side. It wasn't 'invented' until the 1980s, and that was only by some doctors who were doing some research about stress incontinence. But then in 2014 a bunch of Italian scientists decided that we don't have a G-spot at all, and started referring to it as the CUV region,[14] or clitourethrovaginal region, which, I don't know about you, I find a bit tricky to pull off when I'm talking dirty. Others refer to it as the urethral sponge as, according to a book I found really useful called *Women's Anatomy of Arousal*, it's a spongy tube of erectile tissue which swells when aroused.

I was discovering that there are/could be many different types of orgasms, not only clitoral and G-spot, but also cervical, ejaculation, anterior fornix orgasm, posterior fornix orgasm, anal, throat, urethra, whole body, nipple, breath- and energy-gasms, dreamgasms, megagasms, microgasms.

But out of all of these the one that really surprised me was the cervical orgasm. Historically, when someone said 'cervix' I did not think 'sexy fun time'. I thought smear test, cervical cancer or someone telling me a birth story. 'I had just left the Indian restaurant and my cervix was seven centimetres dilated . . .' (Or in my case, panting on all fours screaming, 'I'm in agony! AGONY! I must be fully dilated' and the midwife measuring me and informing me that it was just the one centimetre.) I don't think it's just me that was surprised to find out you could have a cervical orgasm. Even Wikipedia doesn't mention it.

The cervix is the entrance to the womb, found at the top of the vagina. Now, I think I had always thought that it was MILES AND MILES UP THERE and was actually a tiny little entry point or doorway. But again, I was wrong. It is in fact another tube a few inches long. So you have the vaginal passage that leads to the closed cervical passage (it opens when you have a baby), which leads to the womb or uterus. The lower part of the cervix bulges into the vagina. It didn't even occur to me that I could touch my own cervix, but in actual fact, with a bit of gentle poking around and a long finger, I can.

But Google told me that cervical orgasms are THE SHIT! Words like 'powerful', 'mystical', 'ecstasy' are bandied around in relation to the cervical orgasm. I'm not exaggerating here, there are sex vloggers and teachers who testify that cervical orgasms are a life-changing, wonderful experience. *Cosmopolitan* magazine has a vivid description:[15]

> The cervix is the reflexology point for the heart. Stimulating it will cause very intense feelings of love and spiritual transcendence. It's like taking the feelings you have when you first fall in love, and multiplying that by ten. Or you know how you feel after you've had a really good cry? Every cell in your being feels cleansed and revitalised. You feel like you are floating and in extreme bliss. The effects of it can last for hours and even days.

Wowzers.

Have a lookie in the box below here for some more info about each type of orgasm when you get a second.

The rest of the orgasm menu

Ejaculation
Taoist texts from the fourth century mention female ejaculation, as does the ancient Indian *Kama Sutra*, and nowadays it's splashing out all over the place in online porn. Researchers Beverley Whipple and John D. Perry

found out that the stimulation of the G-spot (or CUV region) can result in this squirting of . . . oh, here's another bloomin' controversy, some say it's wee, some say it isn't. All I know is that there can be a bit of it or a proper soggy-bed sized amount of fluid. But while Western academics are quibbling over what the fluid is, tantric people are LOVING it, whatever it is, as you can tell by the name they give it, *amrita*, which means nectar of the gods.[16]

Vaginal orgasm

A vaginal orgasm, as the name would suggest, is an orgasm that comes from stimulation within the vagina.

The A-spot – anterior fornix – orgasm

Or as I like to call it, 'the bit that is a bit higher up than the G-spot' orgasm. From what I can gather, the A-spot, (also sometimes referred to as the deep spot) is all the way up the belly side of your vagina, beyond the G-spot, before but near the cervix. I had never heard of it. Apparently, according to an article I read and enjoyed in *Vice*, it was discovered by a sex educator and pleasure coach, awesomely named Glamazon Tyomi, who discovered her A-spot while with a partner.[17] 'I began to realize how moist I would become in certain positions when my partner was deep. The increase in wetness would also come with a warm, calming, euphoric feeling across my body, and I noticed that it would happen with deep penetration near my cervix . . . I knew this wasn't something that was commonly experienced or discussed, so I began to do research.'

Posterior fornix or deep-spot orgasm

Or as I call it, the 'bit higher up and on the other side of the

G-spot' orgasm. From what I can glean, when the vagina is aroused, it can balloon to open up a new area just below and behind the cervix, which can be known as the cul de sac, and is said to be incredible when stimulated or reached with the tip of a penis. I got a bit muddled when reading articles about this online though, because, confusingly, some sexperts refer to the anterior fornix as being the deep spot, while for others it is the posterior fornix.

Anal orgasm

Calling it an anal orgasm is a bit of a misnomer, as from what I can glean, while it's certainly possible to have an orgasm when having anal sex, it's not an anal orgasm as such, but more likely owing to indirect stimulation of the G-spot or clitoris or even the posterior fornix.[18] It could even be an energy-gasm (which we'll come to in a moment).

Mouth and throat orgasm

Some say there is a throat clit. I have to say I doubted this one, thinking it was part of some sort of blowjob conspiracy – especially as when you do an internet search for throat orgasm you get pages and pages of blowjob videos. *What? Women have a throat clit but not men? What do you take us for?* But an academic fella called Herbert Otto, in his 1999 study *Liberated Orgasm: the Orgasmic Revolution,* found that both women and men can orgasm from the mouth. The mouth is a primary erotic zone with the capacity for triggering its own unique orgasms. The sensations usually start in the lips, tongue, or roof of the mouth or throat. Intense feelings of pleasure build up in the lips and then at the point of release, a full-body orgasm is experienced. Men were less likely to want to talk about them, though.[19]

The U-spot (urethra – pee-hole) orgasm

There is a patch of erectile tissue either side of and above a woman's urethra, which, according to *Cosmopolitan*, can be lovely when gently stimulated.[20]

Whole-body orgasm

This is when your whole body vibrates with orgasmic energy. It doesn't have to have anything to do with genital touching, as you might expect. There are many videos online of people giving and receiving these and they do look a bit odd, I have to say, and as though some magic is at work. The people in the videos are generally clothed and one of them sits up and waves their arms over another person who is lying down; at some point the person on the floor starts writhing and howling. This apparently is a whole-body orgasm, and can make the recipient feel alive, tingly and as though they have experienced a big energetic release. Curious.

Breast/nipple orgasm

Research on non-genital orgasms in 2011 discovered that stimulation of the nipple activates an area of the brain called the genital sensory cortex, which is the same region activated by stimulation of the clitoris, vagina and cervix.[21] So it would appear that women's brains process nipple and genital stimulation in the same way. Therefore, it can often be the case that women love breast play and stimulation and can even orgasm from it. I think I had got pretty close to experiencing this myself before.

Breath- or energy-gasm

These tend to be more often acknowledged in tantra and New Age circles rather than in mainstream culture. They can be brought on by focused, deep rhythmical breathing. You build energy with your breath, altering your state of consciousness, and often initiating a release of energy/ change in consciousness, which can be pretty intense.

Blended orgasms or combination-gasms
A sort of mix and match of any of the above.

Megagasm
As far as I can tell, this term was coined by my favourite sexpert, Annie Sprinkle. Let's quote from the brilliant book she wrote with Beth Stephens, *The Explorer's Guide to Planet Orgasm*:

> During a megagasm it can feel as if a lifetime of pent-up emotion were bursting free – and it is. Your body feels open, with electricity streaming through. You may experience lots of tingling in your hands and lips, your jaw may chatter and your lover may end up having some kind of contact orgasm too. Just hold on tight, and ride, ride, ride that humongous wild tidal wave of bliss.[22]

In her documentary *Sluts and Goddesses*, Sprinkle is filmed having a five-minute megagasm. I'll just repeat that: A FIVE-MINUTE MEGAGASM. It is indeed mega. I dig Annie Sprinkle.

Microgasm
Annie Sprinkle also talks about microgasms. If we tap away our thoughts right now we can 'focus on our erotic energy body, and visualise the orgasmic flow inside us' and bring on orgasmic feelings.[23] Don't dismiss it as

woo-woo, I became aware of this when I was holidaying with the Germans and they kept asking me how I was feeling in my body. Often I felt a little 'orgasm-y', as though little currents were moving through my body and I was bobbing away with them, like a moored boat. It was through these currents that I could feel the hints and essence of orgasm.

The more I thought about it the more I found it a mindscrew that there was an awesome world of pleasure not even as far away as my doorstep, and I'd never bothered to *really* explore it. It was as though I'd been to a football match but not thought to watch the game. There were many hints that the match was important, all the signs, arrows and noise, but I'd just sat and had a cup of tea by the entrance and bought a scarf. There had been clues all along that my cunt was an important area – starting with the fact that cunts are basically the gateway to life, where we 'make love' and make babies. Pretty significant as far as areas go. I should have cottoned on to it sooner, got to know it, love it. I should have built a bloomin' altar to my pleasure dome! Instead I'd been spending my time getting pissed and worrying about the size of my bottom. Still, at least I was now on a mission to change all that.

I consulted my (somewhat random) fornication library for hints on what I should be doing masturbation-wise. I'd been amassing a fair few books on sex since I'd had the idea to go on my sexual odyssey. I enjoyed popping into bookshops and confidently asking, 'Where are your books on sex?' Most of the time salespeople would look at each other, squint and whisper, 'I'm not sure, do we have any?' before helping me to locate the three books on sex (two on the *Kama Sutra* and one called something like *365 Tips to Spice up your Sex Life*) in the corner of the pregnancy section.

Strange, is it not, that as a society we do far more sex than golf or drawing and yet you can fill your boots with books about golf and drawing, but not sex. And don't think to yourself, 'Well of course not, if you want a book on sex go to a sex shop,' because they tend not to sell books about how to become a masterful lover either. Ann Summers has a few, but it is still NOTHING compared to the number of books you can purchase in any bookshop on, say, military history or colouring-in.

Anyway, in the book *Ultimate Sex* by Anne Hooper, bought on sale in a bookshop in Brighton, thank you very muchly, two pages with pictures were devoted to a woman self-pleasuring. Her wanks bore absolutely no resemblance to mine and it wasn't just that she had done her hair. She didn't have her jeans on and she wasn't even using a laptop. She was caressing her naked body all over before getting involved with her erogenous zones, and when she did she slid her fingers inside herself and everything. I'd never done that.

It appeared that not only should I be loving myself in a 'you're all right, you know, Luce' type of way but I should also be *making* a wee bit of love to myself too. Me and myself should be getting it awwwn.

So, keen student that I was, I got practising. I earmarked some time here and there for wanking practice and oh, I hadn't had so much fun in a long time. 'I just gave myself the most amazing orgasm,' I practised telling the vegans, feeling like some sort of emancipated sex goddess.

My new wanking technique

I tidied my room, for starters
OK, less a tidy, more a 'hide the mess' – I'd take the books, hangers and plates off my bed and make it. You get the gist.

I washed
Yep, had a bath. Cleaned my bits. I know how to treat a lady.

I orchestrated some subtle lighting, lit the smelly candle I got for my birthday, that kind of thing

I turned off Radio 1 and put on some relaxing spa-type music

I kicked off proceedings by lying still on the bed for a while
Maybe I was tired after all the tidying, or perhaps I was simply listening to what my body wanted and it was telling me to slow the feck down. But I lay there with my eyes closed, hands resting between my boobs, or on my belly, and my knees sprawled outwards, soles of the feet touching. It was an unintentionally Zen pose. I ended up lying like this for quite some time. I liked it. I relaxed. It was as if all the bits of me that had scattered throughout the day returned. It was here that I began to *feel* my body after all that stomping about in my head and thoughts.

I started by caressing myself
I simply saw where and how my body wanted to be touched. Sometimes I'd like to feel the lightest of touches over my hands, arms and neck. The gentlest of strokes on my neck and the inside of my arms are lovely. Or maybe I'd massage my scalp, pull my ear lobes, give myself a good knead. Whatever I did it felt as though I was waking my whole body up.

I'd try to tap thoughts away when they popped into my mind
Thoughts like: 'Look at you! Lolling about stroking your elbow!' or, 'Shit, that book I took out of the library at Easter! What did I do with it?' I'd do a little 'jog on please, little thought' or 'Luce, shut the feck up' – whatever seemed appropriate.

I spent a long time massaging my breasts

Diana Richardson, of the tantra book *The Heart of Tantric Sex*, talks about feeling from the inside of the breasts, breathing into the breasts and noticing what sensations happen inside the body there. That alone is a lovely relaxing thing to do. I would stay like that for a little while and then move on to exploring the sensitivity of my nipples, teasing and pinching them, often building a fair bit of arousal here.

Touching your boobs!

Key points to remember:
- Don't go straight for a nipple grab!
- Take your time and tease yourself as much as possible.
- Follow your intuition and touch yourself how you want to be touched.

With or without oil, use your hands and fingers to explore your belly, ribs, shoulders, top of chest, and the space between your breasts. Then work your way around the breasts. Rest for as long as you like there, breathing into your breasts, perhaps cupping them very gently. Then start to give yourself some touch in this area, starting light like a feather and moving on to longer and firmer strokes, making sure you don't get to the areola until you are excited to do so. Then gently explore the areola, lightly kneading and stroking the area, tuning in to what feels good. Start with very light touch on the nipple itself. You might like to tease yourself – as you start to get aroused pull away and explore the outer breasts again or the belly, and then work your way back again. Keep edging like this to build sensation and sexual energy.

I like pinching and pulling at the nipples ever so gently and then slowly releasing them. As you get more and more aroused you will be able to handle stronger pinches and they will feel great. From this firmer pinch, you can then bring in little twists. You can keep pulling away when very aroused to build pleasure. You may find your vagina contracts and you orgasm from nipple and breast touch alone. Or you may like to include some vulva and vagina touch. Follow what your body wants. Enjoy!! X

I started to very gently feel my vulva
I'd use a bit of the vegans' coconut oil from the fridge (sorry, guys, I did take it out with a spoon) and spit to keep the area very wet, and then I'd just have a bit of a feel, going wherever I was drawn. I love the smoothness of the skin around my vagina, and I loved the sensations when I massaged and pressed the area towards the back near the perineum. I'd let myself have a good old wander. Sometimes I'd realise I was moving in a certain way, I might be tickling or tapping myself, say, and I'd be surprised, as though I hadn't really been conscious of how I'd ended up doing what I was doing.

What I found with the clitoris (well, not so much the 'proverbial' clitoris as my own clitoris) was that it was too much if I went straight there but wonderful if I'd built up sensation around the area beforehand.

Also my clitoris loved wetness: spit, dribble, oil or lube. A dry finger straight to my clitoris was uncomfortable, if not sore, but with a good build-up and lots of wetness it became very much 'yeah, baby!' So I would very slowly, gently and rhythmically feel around and on my clitoris and then the pressure and speed would naturally increase, my body would contort rather wonderfully, and I could bring myself to an orgasm this way.

But I found that if I orgasmed by stimulating just my clitoris then afterwards I would feel 'done' and pretty much off the sex thing. Therefore, more and more I found myself holding back from orgasming with my clitoris alone. I might build the pleasure there, but what I found really exciting was when I experienced this clitoral arousal alongside stimulation inside the vagina.

I touched my G-spot

Myths abounded that it was VERY HARD to find the G-spot and before, when I'd had a little ferret around for it, I was never entirely sure if I had it or not. The problem for me was in the title. The word spot confused me, and I felt I should be looking for a dot-like mark somewhere in the vagina that would holler 'whamalamadingdong!' when it was discovered.

However, now, with my slooooow build-up, and following the trail of my body, I very soon became acquainted with it. I had thought my G-spot was way up there and would need a hard hat and torch to find, but it was practically just inside my vagina. It wasn't such a big deal to locate; I found that if I took my time touching myself and my clitoris was aroused, when I put a finger inside myself it would naturally find a bumpy area and cling to it. I would feel my vagina contracting around my finger. And then, shit me, now we're talking, my orgasms took on a whole other dimension. They became deeper, longer, richer.

I found the G-spot to be not so much a spot as an area, and it really does ring true that it is a urethral sponge, as it feels like a tube. But nothing at all happens unless I'm aroused elsewhere. If I just pop a finger in now it will do nothing for me sexually – it will just feel uncomfortable and a tiny bit unpleasant. But if I stroke my body, massage my breasts and nipples, explore the area around my clitoris, add a bit of gentle clit touch, and THEN add the finger, well, helloooooo, me!

More and more I was learning that I needed a warming-up period but that after this bit of limbering up, well . . . I was a wild and wanton wanker.

I called my lovely self-pleasure sessions my 'tantric wanks' (I should probably apologise to the tantric community for doing so) and I've even created a handy bullet-point guide to the tantric wank, so you can have a go yourself, pin it on the bathroom door or send a copy to Auntie Sheila.

Ten steps to a tantric wank

1. **Tidy your wanking palace**
   You're not lying on an unmade bed waiting for something to buffer now! Pick up your socks and put them in the laundry bin. The tantric wank has style!
2. **Wash your bits**
   Go on, honky, you've been weeing all day. Get carried away! Have a bath!
3. **Light a smelly candle**
   You know, that one you got for your birthday – you're worth it.
4. **Pour yourself a little something**
   A nice chilled glass of whatever you fancy. Sauvignon blanc? Irn-Bru? Milk? Just a little glass, no need to consume ten pints and a shot of sambuca to make love to yourself.
5. **Press play**
   A bit of Marvin Gaye? Ed Sheeran? Black Lace? Whatever tickles your fancy.
6. **Get undressed**
   Sod it, take it all off. The tantric wank says you can't

make love to yourself in a pair of Primark jeans and a T-shirt that says 'Sarah's Hen Do – Bournemouth' with a picture of Sarah, aged five, standing in a toilet dressed as a pirate.

7. **Close your eyes, relax and breathe**
   Yeah, man, do some of that crazy breathing shit! Yeah, baby. Breathe, feel sexy, feel beautiful, feel like the best lover in the world . . .

8. **Don't touch your bits yet**
   What are you? A Labrador in a hurry? Caress yourself, all over, mmmm mmmm mmmmm . . . the tantric wank, who sounds like Barry White, says, 'We're making *lurve* here.'

9. **You can touch your bits now**
   But no rubbing or yanking . . . the tantric wank, who incidentally now sounds like the Caramel Bunny, says, 'Take it slow.'

10. **Orgasm – blow all of your fuses at once and trip off into space!**
    See! See how the tantric wank yields a much higher calibre of orgasm!! Yee-haaaw! And, there's more, yes, because the tantric wank is the wank that keeps on giving . . . it won't be followed by the 'DELETE MY COMPUTER HISTORY NOW!' alarm you feel post internet porn wank.

The really important thing for me in this self-pleasure practice was that I didn't try to get anywhere. It seemed that the less I 'thought', the better it was. So instead of setting out saying, 'Today I'm going to have a crack at the posterior fornix orgasm,' I simply let my body lead itself and focused on what I was experiencing.

The orgasm that could create world peace

So, with all this exploring . . . what did I find? Orgasms. Oh yes. Oh ho ho. YES!!! My orgasms transformed completely. Rather than a few seconds of throbbing and contractions, my orgasms became whole journeys where sensations and energy careered throughout my whole body. I wasn't always able to ascertain what sort of orgasm I was having – I think I mostly had, and still do have, blended gasms – but isolating the different areas and ticking orgasms off a list didn't really bother me. To be honest, I was just happy to experience whatever occurred, as it tended to be pretty high up there on the wow scale. However, there was one orgasm which stands out, so much so I've given it the understated nickname of 'the orgasm that could create world peace'.

I was alone in bed one night. The lights were off, but the curtains were open and I could see the stars. (I'm so romantic.) I started exploring my body gently. As usual, I slowly built up my pleasure, stimulating my nipples, giving myself a moist massage of the labia and clitoris, and then placing my fingers inside myself, my body moving and writing and bouncing as it fancied. Nothing was particularly out of the ordinary, but the orgasm reached a zenith I had never experienced before and I felt like I rode a wave of pleasure for, blimey, I don't know how long, but there were a fair few good long minutes. I want to use the word 'mind-blowing' but if I do I'll have to apologise for all the previous times I've used the word 'mind-blowing', because I'd never felt anything like this before. It felt as though these pleasurable sensations were coming from deep within me, but I was so massive that my centre was the middle of the earth or something. Even when this peak subsided I was still in an orgasmic state; I could feel it as I went to sleep. Indeed, I was still feeling the effects of this orgasm at dinner time the following day, and my body STILL echoed with these pleasant opening, throbbing sensations the day after that.

But the reason I call it 'the orgasm that could create world peace' is because of what happened as I was coming down from the peak. I lay back in all these waves of pleasure as though I was being whisked through worlds and space and time. And words were coming into my head somehow, though they didn't feel like normal thoughts – I don't think I was able to have normal thoughts as I was so *in* this physical experience – anyway, it seemed as though I was being given a message, and it went something along these lines: *This is it, this is the secret that has been lost, this is the key.*

Yes, OK, go for it, say I've lost my mind. But actually I do think there is something in these words.

Women are capable of powerful, transcendent pleasure, but that fact has not just been lost, it hasn't been respected at all. Women's sexual power has been suppressed, feared, denied and punished over thousands of years, and women have been murdered and mutilated because of it.

I became both fascinated and horrified by all of this. The sheer scale of time that women and their sexual power, pleasure and freedom have been repressed floored me. I couldn't stop thinking about it and spent weeks and weeks at my computer compiling a timeline, which is at the back of this book, as I tried to get my head around it all.

But back to the orgasm: if I had to classify it, it would probably be a megagasm, or maybe a cervical orgasm. I wasn't aware that I had stimulated my cervix at the time, but I certainly identify with the reverential tone I've noticed in descriptions of the feelings that cervical orgasms prompt, such as 'intense feelings of love and spiritual transcendence' (Kim Anami)[24] and 'a depth of soul, emotion and physical power that it is hard to describe' (Kendal Williams).[25]

Ejaculation

I may have been a tad thrifty with the truth when I said I simply listened to where my body wanted to go when I masturbated and didn't set out with an agenda to specifically experience one orgasm or another. It was nearly true.

Yes, my wanking had become divine and delicious, and I was thrilled that I could surf my own pleasure and experience a whole gamut of wonderful sensations. But there was one orgasm that I became fixated on achieving: female ejaculation, known in porn as 'squirting'.

Yes, all my 'I'll just see where my body wants to be touched' ideas went out of the window when it came to squirting – then I was all DVDs, towels, jerking hand movements, squinting looks of intense concentration and thoughts like, 'I'm going to nail this one if it's all I do!'

I became fascinated by squirting and could frequently be found perusing the offerings on female ejaculation that internet pornography proposed.

In case you were wondering, these hunts for nuggets of squirting wisdom usually looked like this:

Enter big free porn site
Dodge ads for things like 'First Free Pussy Finder', with the pithy tagline 'just search for pussy in your area and ask to fuck' (with an alarming cartoon of a man who looked like he'd got his penis stuck in a woman from behind and was trying to pull it out to no avail), or 'Slut Roulette – come jerk off with random hotties', or 'Free Extreme Porn, Punishtube'. 'Free Extreme Porn, Punishtube' is a bit of a bugger because hardcore excerpts of porn pop up on your screen before you can stop them. It's a bit like going to a restaurant, examining the menu and the chef suddenly appearing and stuffing a bit of liver in your mouth without your

consent. Not the best analogy, I know, but you get the gist. I don't like liver.

Either attempt to ignore ads or take the piss out of them
Imagine there are prestigious porn advertising awards. 'Aaaaaand the winner is *Slut Roulette – come jerk off with random hotties*! The judges were moved by the powerful and meaningful way words and images work together here to arouse the viewer.' Spend time wondering whether there are actually porn advertising awards, with contestants proudly striving to be the shittest.

Check out squirting movies
Porn, as ever, delivers a mixed reticule. Film #1 opens with a topless woman, wearing knickers and a dog collar, writhing around on a sofa licking an item of clothing, not sure what, possibly a sock. She sucks her fingers, turns over and starts slapping her bottom. Three men appear and, in a speedy manoeuvre that must be applauded as a slick bit of choreography, one puts his penis in her vagina, one in her anus and one in her mouth. We are one minute and thirty-five seconds in. Blimey. Look for another video.

Film #2: *Ultima Squirting Pussy*
Over 9 million views. Man and woman kissing on rug by a fire. He performs cunnilingus. She says 'fuck yeah' a lot. Woman's legs are behind her head. (Remind self to do yoga.) She is pinned down by his hands against the bed. Video isn't very good quality. Hard to work out what is going on, think he has two fingers inside her and is moving them back and forward quickly as though unjamming a drawer. More 'fuck yeahs'. Suddenly she squirts everywhere. Wow. Everywhere.

Advert pops up asking me if I would like to fuck a single mom who lives near me

I persevere; third time lucky and all that

Film #3. Starts with young woman, guy is holding the camera and saying 'Sexy bitch, let's see your pussy . . . that's a good girl. That's a good girl,' etc.

This video bears a lot of familiar porn tropes:

- A man is steering the proceedings.
- A man carries the camera. The whole thing is made from the point of view of the male.
- The woman in the film wears very high shoes.
- The woman has no pubic hair.
- There is a blowjob where the woman's head is repeatedly pushed into a big erect penis.
- For most of it the woman doesn't really say anything except for, 'Oh my God.'

But – and this is a really interesting 'but' – because this film is about female squirting, the woman holds the magic 'money' shots, and this slightly alters the normal porn dynamic. While the woman in the video mainly only says, 'Oh my God,' she is heard at one point saying, 'Oh yeah, there. Keep going. Keep going,' that is, instructing the man, and at another point when they are having intercourse he pulls out so she can ejaculate, then he tries to penetrate her again but she says, 'Wait.' Two tiny moments, but they are so striking because it is so rare to hear and see a woman saying what she wants and how she wants it in porn. HURRAH, I say, which is a bit sad really considering these moments are so tiny.

I think I might have been distracting myself from having a go with my practical squirting mission by looking at porn, and now here I am, deviating from telling you about my practical squirting missions by talking about porn. I think there could be something here. Porn, in this case, and I think in other periods of my life, has actually distracted me from experiencing my own sexuality and pleasure.

To be fair, there isn't much to tell about my practical missions in this area, except that I found that when I set out to ejaculate I didn't. But when I gave myself lots of time, say a nice hour, to touch myself wherever I wanted, quite often towards the end of that time, after a few orgasms, I would naturally find myself doing something akin to the jammed-drawer manoeuvre. I would sometimes wonder whether I had ejaculated a bit, but I have never, as yet, gone the full-on jet wash.

There was one time, though, after a particularly glorious boffing session with the Dark-Haired German, where we had been in the yab-yum position (him sitting cross-legged, and me sitting on his lap, with my legs around him). Nice position, although it does get me thinking about my slouch. We finished and both realised that the bed was sopping wet. A proper 'someone has wet themselves' wet.

'What is it?' I screamed genteelly. 'It smells of fox piss!'

Not that I have ever smelled fox piss, I just thought it seemed a bit muskier than cat pee, and I know about cat pee, as my sister's cat once weed on my pillow.

'I think you must have ejaculated,' he said.

The session had been all manner of orgasm-tastic and I had absolutely no idea when the wet puddle came about.

'All that practising and then I do it and don't even realise!' I puffed. 'Humph.'

Speaking up

While we are spinning through galaxies and time in post-orgasmic bliss here, I must tell you about something else which was going on in my life at this point. It is something that serves to show how discovering all this about my own personal and sexual power had changed my life in quite a dramatic way.

I had started a campaign. It was called No More Page 3, and was asking the most popular newspaper in Britain, the *Sun*, to stop showing pictures of topless women every day. As you can probably tell, before this point in my life I hadn't been particularly confrontational or assertive. About anything. And I had certainly never campaigned for anything before. No one was more surprised than me. Well, maybe my mum.

I had finally found my voice, not only in intimate relationships but also out in the world. I guess you could say I was discovering my own power. It was quite extraordinary.

The more I delved into the subject of women and what we learn about ourselves, our power and our sexuality from the culture and society we live in, the more I kept coming up against Page 3, and I just couldn't see how it was doing women any favours. I felt it had fucked me up a bit. As a little girl the message about women that Page 3 communicated every day was really hard for me to navigate. It seemed to say: 'shut up and get your tits out'; 'it's what you look like that matters'; 'you are here for sex with men'. Because it was in the newspaper, it seemed to be normal, and sanctioned by society. The pictures of men in the paper, on the other hand, showed them, well, doing all sorts of things. The message to boys was: 'you can be in business, rule the country, play sports, and do all of this wearing clothes'.

Page 3 was launched in 1970, which was a totally different time. Women had only had equal voting rights to men for forty-two years, and it was legal for a man to rape his wife (I shit you not). The *Sun* was just one newspaper in a male-managed media in a male-dominated society (there were only twenty-six female

MPs out of 630 in 1970). But now we were in the twenty-first century, and I felt sure we had moved on.

So, to start with I wrote a letter to Dominic Mohan, who was the editor of the *Sun* at the time, asking him to please drop the pictures. It was quite long. Three pages, in fact. And it was a pretty good letter, but I knew it wouldn't do anything. He was hardly likely to say, 'She's right! I never want to see another uncovered breast in the *Sun* again!' But I was really curious about whether I was the only one who felt like this, so I started an online petition with change.org, a Facebook group and a Twitter account to find out. I called the campaign No More Page 3 and even had T-shirts printed with those words on.

People soon started telling me that Page 3 had been a source of discomfort and pain for them too. One little girl thanked me because she hated going to her grandad's house and hearing him talk about the Page 3 'girls'. Many said that from a young age they'd drawn jumpers on the Page 3 girls, not knowing exactly why, simply feeling that it wasn't right that there should be a naked young woman in the paper. Women who remembered previous attempts to get rid of these pictures and couldn't believe they were still there wrote to lend their support. I heard from women who had been raped and sexually assaulted, and charities that worked to end violence against women gave their support. This is what Rape Crisis (England and Wales) said:

> The everyday, casual misogyny of Page 3 undoubtedly contributes to our culture in which the objectification of women is completely normalised. Its implicit message is that women's bodies exist chiefly for men's use and consumption. This is the wider context in which 80,000 women are raped and over 400,000 sexually assaulted in England and Wales each year.
>
> We within the Rape Crisis movement see the devastating impacts of this gender-based sexual violence daily. Page 3 has no public-service role and no place in a publication calling itself a newspaper. The time for it to go is long overdue.[26]

I had read the statistic that one in four women will experience sexual assault in their lifetime and I'd initially thought, 'Oh no, that's too high.' But then I remembered the experience in my early twenties which I mentioned earlier, where I had gone with a friend to stay at her friend's house after a party. I had gone to bed, alone, and fallen asleep. A little while later I woke up. My top had been lifted up and a man's hand was moving inside my pants. He was kneeling over me, his penis in his other hand. Wanking over me. I jumped up and made for the door. The guy was mortified. 'Stay, stay,' he was saying. I left. It was the middle of the night. I walked miles through London to get home. I stayed inside with the curtains drawn for three days after that. Shocked. I hardly mentioned it to anyone. I made sure I never saw the guy again. I had been asleep. I had gone to bed on my own. No consent was given. At all. And yet, afterwards, I had a sense that somehow it must have been my fault. That I should have known better. That I shouldn't have been there. I told one friend about it at the time. She told me she had been raped but she hadn't really told anyone about that either.

I began speaking more about this, and asking women if they had had any similar experiences. I rarely spoke to a woman who didn't have a story of some sort of sexual coercion, assault or trauma. More often than not, women told me a litany of them. It was sobering, saddening. But I think we were also empowered by sharing these stories, as though finally we felt validated that it wasn't our fault after all. It wasn't *us* in the wrong. So powerful had the public narrative of victim blaming been around sexual violence against women that accusations like 'She was asking for it', 'Well, she shouldn't drink like that', 'Did you see what she was wearing, what do you expect?' was all we heard. We had never heard, 'He shouldn't have done that'; 'He should have known better'. A collective penny was dropping: 'Er, we were taught not to get ourselves raped . . . shouldn't someone have told the boys not to rape?'

In 2012, a young woman called Laura Bates started a website called Everyday Sexism, where people could share their own experiences of sexism. She was staggered by the response. Social media had given everyone a voice. And women were using it. Bloody hell, we were using it. We didn't feel alone with this stuff any more. 'That happened to me!' 'I've always hated that.' 'Me too!' Women were coming together. And it felt like coming home.

But men were speaking up as well! The lovely men! So many started championing the No More Page 3 petition. One man made me cry with an email: 'I'm sitting here with my seven-month-old daughter, thinking what an important job it is you're doing.' Men who confided that they were addicted to internet porn wrote and thanked me for taking a stand about the way it's seen as normal to show women as sexual objects everywhere.

I did get a fair bit of shit too on social media, sad to say. I got death threats. I was told to 'fuck off you've got crap tits' in a variety of ways, which made me chuckle, to be honest. There was I, who for years and years had told myself I had shit boobs and shit everything else, but had now got to a point of loving my boobs, my body, my me, only for a load of tosspots to tell me the contrary. I also got told to 'get a life' a lot. That was ironic because this journey I found myself on made me feel more as though my life was a gift and an adventure than I'd ever felt before.

Oh, and I was told I was frigid, a prude and a killjoy for speaking against Page 3. Interesting, I thought, that these were old-fashioned-sounding words. A language of sexual bullying, of being pushed towards something that you don't want to do or aren't ready for, was still deeply ingrained in our society. At first I was surprised by the sexism, the put-downs and attempts to belittle or silence me, but it only proved my point, and made me work a little bit harder.

It also reminded me how restrictive our narrative around sex was for women. As a woman, I felt that my sexuality had been presented to me by men for my whole life. Page 3, lads' mags, online porn: most of this content was devised by men for men. No wonder I had found myself in my thirties a bit lost when it came to sex.

Many pro-Page 3 people used to tell me that Page 3 was empowering for women, and I did get why they said that. I absolutely understand how it might make a woman feel powerful, to be picked because she was deemed pretty, with nice boobs, and then to have a big picture of herself in the newspaper and to be paid for it. But saying that Page 3 was empowering to women always seem seemed a strange argument to me – as though people had thought to themselves, 'Hmmm, have you noticed that girls and young women seem quite disempowered, they don't speak up, they are getting a lot of sexual abuse and they have pretty bad self-images? You know what I think would really empower them? If in the newspaper we showed big pictures of young women showing their bare boobs!'

But I did see women, like myself, being empowered by finding feminism and speaking up against Page 3 and other issues. Women I campaigned with said they kept discovering skills they didn't know they had; they would find themselves organising events, talking to big businesses, writing, speaking publicly. Many went on to study, write books, start campaigns, step into politics and pursue careers they loved.

None of this is to say that feminist campaigning is quick and easy. It took two and a half years for the *Sun* to drop the feature. But it felt, and it still does feel, as though the universe was on our side, behind women, and egging us on to step into our power and start shaping the world how we would like.

BELL TENTS AND OTHER SURPRISES

Not forsaking all others

The Dark-Haired German had made it clear from the outset that he wouldn't move to Blighty. He loved Germany and had a house and career over there. I was the self-employed writer, so the onus was on me to relocate. But the thing is, I can't imagine living anywhere else but England. Well, except maybe in a coastal Californian cabin for a while. Ooo yes, with an open fire . . . I could write a book and finally do some yoga . . .

What was I saying? Oh yes, that I'd never leave Britain. Because much as elements of the place can annoy me – a political system where lots of men stand in a sealed chamber baying at each other, computerised tills in the supermarkets and all that jazz – I just sort of, well, feel British. I get the humour, and this is where my history and all my points of reference are. I really liked Germany, but I couldn't imagine living there. I always seemed to get told off for cycling or walking in the wrong place, or talking when I shouldn't. It's not like in England where people get passively annoyed with you – there they do it actively. It's very unnerving when you're not used to it.

I tended to go over there rather than the other way around

because he lived in an actual house on his own, while I lived in a flat full of vegans and had a room with sloping ceilings, which meant that there was only one point right in the middle of the room where he could stand up fully – a fact I rather enjoyed, as it meant we lay down a lot.

Anyway, on one of my visits over there, we were having a cup of tea shortly after I arrived when he, the Dark-Haired German, nonchalantly dropped this biggie: 'So, I have been on a date with someone. We didn't get physical, but I would like to. I think more and more I could be in two relationships,' he said, and offered me a biscuit.

'Oh wow, that's fascinating,' I responded. 'Open relationships are all the rage. The relationships of the future. I'm happy if you're happy.' I smiled. 'Lovely biscuits.'

Luuuuucy. The truth.

Yes, well, it's hard to remember my exact words. But I uttered an asphyxiated response along the lines of, 'OHMY GOODNESSOHMYGOODNESSOHMYGOODNESS!!! I can't believe what you just said! How could you do this to me??? I'm going to fly home.'

Lots of crying as I booked a flight. Texted friend: 'You'll never guess what he's done to me,' etc, etc. Had some pretty intense, emotional, INCREDIBLE sex. Got to the airport. Flew home. Masturbated on the aeroplane. (I know. I was all of a tither.)

But, um, the next part is a bit embarrassing. Because once I'd got home, and had called him a bastard to all my friends, who firmly and repeatedly told me he wasn't good enough for me, I calmed down. And when I stopped with the dramatics and tuned into myself, a strange thing happened. I realised that the idea wasn't so bad after all. Actually, it was quite a good idea that suited me perfectly. Yes, if he saw this other woman, who had sounded very nice indeed, then I wouldn't worry so much that I wasn't able to give him all the attention he needed. Also, he was such a good lover, I liked the thought that another woman could have all that pleasure as well. And, wow, I noticed that the thought of him giving pleasure to someone else quite turned me on, too. The whole situation suddenly felt like a massive win to me. This was one way that we could stay together rather than break up.

Yet my outraged response had been so instant and automated. If a guy tells you he wants to see someone else that's what you do, you feel 'betrayed', 'wronged', 'spurned'; she is the 'other woman', 'the better/younger model'; you are the 'victim', 'devastated', 'broken-hearted'; he is 'a total bastard'. Had all that just been a script I'd picked up from pop songs, played out dramatically even when it didn't represent what I actually felt?

The situation was curious and confusing, but in the end I said yes, I would give it a go.

Better bumbling

We carried on for a wee while in this more open relationship. I liked the situation. It felt as though a weight had been lifted from me. I didn't have to be everything for one person, which had felt virtually impossible while I was in another country.

Then the Dark-Haired German met someone who he was really drawn to. He wanted to be free to fall for her and be in an exclusive relationship with her. So we let it go. I was and still am so grateful to him for all I learned with him, and for the experience of being with him for that time.

So on I bumbled on alone. But, if I may say so, I think I was bumbling better than I ever had before. I even asked a man out and did it via email this time rather than in a cagoule at a bus stop. How mature, how assured I'd become. There was a bit of feeling wretched when he said no, but no multiple measured spirits at all.

It was about this time that I met a real life, bona fide, shiny-eyed tantra teacher, Roxana. Which was when it dawned on me that I hadn't really been doing this sexual journeying thing in the most efficient way. Generally, as a rule, if you want to learn something you study it, you know, with a teacher, as opposed to just relying on enthusiasm and an internet connection.

'Have you got any courses coming up?' I asked Roxana.

'Yes, I am doing an intro to tantra couples workshop in a few weeks.'

YES! HURRAH! I was going to become a shiny-eyed goddess too. I wasn't going to let the fact that I wasn't in a couple stop me.

'Amazing!' I whooped.

I asked an old male friend if he would join me on that weekend. Old male friend and I had done a bit of random shagging over the years and always remained buddies. He knew of my current quest and was supportive of it. I asked him by text if he wanted to join me at the workshop, and he said yes. Boom. What I had forgotten, though, is that he was such a good and old friend that he was almost like a brother, and the brotherly aspect of this relationship generally manifested in us doing each other's heads in. We would meet up, get on well, fancy each other, do some snogging or have sex, have an argument, and then not see each other for a while. And on, ad infinitum.

The week before the course was to take place, I got in touch to go through the details.

'But I've got a trip planned for this weekend,' he told me.

'But . . . but what about the tantra course?'

'Ah, oh shit. Forgot. I wasn't sure that was happening.'

'Grrrr!'

I called shiny-eyed tantra woman.

'I now have no partner to come with. I really want to do your course! You don't, by any chance, have a man I could borrow, do you?'

'Er. Right. Well. Yes, I mean maybe. We'll try to find someone for you.'

And she did. A tall and rather handsome German. And I was partial to those! Now, I thought a beginners' tantra weekend would be all eye-gazing and hand-holding; I definitely didn't think there would be anything naked going on. Otherwise I wouldn't have suggested partnering with a stranger. And I'd have worn better pants.

To be fair, going on a couples' tantra course wasn't really my brightest idea. Not that it wasn't interesting to learn more about tantra and do some tantric exercises. But I could imagine how doing these with someone you loved and were in a relationship with could be incredibly powerful.

Take, for example, the very first exercise we did. We sat opposite our partners. One asked the other, 'Why are you here?' The other person answered. Then again the same question was asked and again the same person answered. On it went for minutes and then the roles were reversed. My answers were, 'I'm interested in learning more about tantra'; 'I was inspired by Roxana's shiny-eyedness'; 'I'm curious about doing sex in a different way,' and that sort of thing. But I imagined how doing that with a partner you had been with for years would have made the stakes so much higher. Telling your long-term partner, 'I want to do sex in a different way,' or, 'I want to feel closer to you,' or 'because you made me,' would pack a punch.

Then there was an exercise where the women got to shout at the men, to unleash any pent-up anger from their life together or for the years of oppression that women had suffered. The men were simply to stand and witness this. I had a go, but felt a bit mean shouting at some poor fella whose name I was still trying to remember. But I had a feeling that doing that with a partner would have been a whole different kettle of kippers altogether.

Then there was the physical aspect. One of the exercises had me straddling this chap in the yab-yum position. We had to breathe, well, pant is a better word for it, really, while some atmospheric rhythmic music played. I was worried I would squash him.

'Are you *sure* you can breathe?' I whispered.

I did quite like the high I got from that breathing though. It reminded me of when I was small, how I would often hold my breath or spin around and around and then bathe in the dizziness or light-headedness afterwards.

We got down to our pants for the last exercise of the last day. One person lay down while the other gently touched them at each chakra point while they breathed into this contact. The chakras are, in Indian thought, the seven centres of spiritual power or energy in the human body. The base chakra point is at the sex area, people! I think I had rather a good go at this exercise. I got down to my knickers, which is no mean feat for someone who generally has a big issue with public nudity. But surrendering to energetic bliss was a long way off. All I could think about was that I hadn't done my bikini line and I should stop washing my light pants with darker colours.

Another terrible handjob

To make up for forgetting about the tantra weekend, old buddy offered to help out in some other way. So I suggested I would like to use his penis for educational purposes. Looking back, I should probably have remembered how we never went for long without infuriating each other.

Before I begin this tale of woe, I would like to take a moment to congratulate myself, because this attempt saw me, Lucy, creating the experience I was seeking rather than blindly bumbling along into it. Tick. Very good. Smiley face. Now back to the story. I invited this old buddy round to my place for a lingam massage. When he agreed, I said, 'Knock on my door at eight o'clock and prepare to get naked.' Yes! Badass. I thank you.

Now, I was pretty busy at the time and my tiny living area wasn't the tidiest. Feminist pamphlets, placards, slogan T-shirts and dirty plates covered all surfaces and floor. Not the soothing erotic space suggested on the tantra websites. I had a bloody good clean, reasoning that if it all went tits up then at least I'd tidied. I even washed myself. I know! I was pulling out all the stops. I got some subtle lighting going – the odd lamp and a bargain pack of tea lights. I laid cushions on the floor and tried to create an intimate boudoir in our small flatshare.

I'd done a lot of homework (lingam massage Google searches on a particularly long train journey). The sites were fairly thorough in telling me how to handle the member in question. I just hoped I could remember it all.

A few moves I thought I'd have a try at:

- The 'pulling the endless handkerchief out of a hat' move: you try to get a smooth motion going, where you pull from the base of the penis up the shaft and off with one hand and then the other, and on and on.
- The 'pull down the rope, sailor' move. Basically the same as the other one but the other direction,
- The 'start a fire' manoeuvre: clamp the penis between two flat hands and then rub them together.
- Juicing a lemon: massage the top of the penis as though you are juicing a lemon.

'Up and up, down and down, start the fire, make some juice,' I muttered as I stowed a bundle of dirty No More Page 3 T-shirts under the bed.

A knock on the door. I was nervous. I let him in and led him in to my room/boudoir/feminist campaigning HQ and sat us both down face to face. The website said to take a few moments first 'breathing together', which is what living humans tend to do when in company, but in this case the breathing was supposed to be an activity in its own right.

'Come on, let's sit down, look in each other's eyes and do some of that crazy breathing shit, yeah baby,' I said.

Oh God, I'd turned into *Flight of the Conchords*. I noticed he seemed quite nervous too. We looked into each other's eyes, smiling, and took some deep breaths. It was far, far, FAR away from the emptying of the mind that moments of meditation should be because my twat self had taken this moment to reappear and was flying round and round my mind like a children's mobile in a horror film screeching, 'Wah, Lucy, you're such a dick,' on a loop. Brilliant. Just brilliant.

'Please take off your clothes and lie down on your front,' I instructed. He undressed. I took my robe off too. Both butt naked. Yikes.

I started to massage his back. The website said I was supposed to spend at least ten minutes relaxing his whole body before I headed to his schlong. Schlong, what a word! I don't know how relaxing he found it. I know I found it pretty bloomin' stressful, mainly because he really annoyed me by telling me where to press. 'There, up a bit, harder, harder, there, ow. Down a bit. Harder. Harder.' It's not a feckin' sports massage! He was supposed to be relaxing and surrendering to my touch, not bossing me about. But I didn't use my 'we should communicate our truths even if they are uncomfortable' trick; I silently seethed instead.

'Turn onto your back,' I said, frostily. He did as he was told. I didn't play with his pecker yet, first I had to massage the rest of him. He was quieter on this side. I started to unwind and even began to enjoy it. Sometimes I closed my eyes as I felt his body beneath my hands, moving slightly to the pulse of the erotic massage playlist I found on Spotify, pithily called 'Sensual Music for Lovers, date night for romantic dinner, spa music for shiatsu and reiki, Kama Sutra music to make love, music for sex'. I kneaded him, stroked him, oh, I'm getting the hang of this now.

And then he said something.

He said something.

'The fuel consumption on that first Transit I had was dreadful,' he said.

I had made no previous reference to Transit vans.

Ever.

'The fuel consumption on that first Transit I had was dreadful.'

I shit you not.

What was I supposed to do with that? It's not even a conversation starter I would be equipped to handle if I was fully clothed and not about to start a fire with someone's penis. Should I just stop? I wanted to give him a little wallop, but I didn't. I continued to massage him for a bit, feeling baffled and distracted. Eventually I thought 'sod it' and stopped.

'Maybe we should just stop this,' I humphed.

He seemed surprised.

'You don't seem into it,' I ventured.

'I am. It was nice.'

Nice! Fecking nice. I was well humphy now.

We had a little cuddle and then eventually I carried on. It got quite fun when we finally arrived at the penis. I remembered the moves, busted them out and yankeedoodle they went down well!

'Oh, that's new,' he panted. 'That's amazing.'

Now she's getting somewhere! Fully in charge of a penis and making rather a good job of it for once!

I was thoroughly enjoying myself. Using lots of oil, having a good play. Penises are great, aren't they? Then something odd happened. Well, I suppose it wasn't that odd, but it certainly changed the vibe. For me anyway. He suddenly stood up, and manoeuvred us towards a big mirror. He was standing and holding his own penis now. I was on my knees swivelling towards him. He wanted to come like that. In my mouth. And I let him. I opened my mouth and he came in it. I guess that was his happy ending. Only I didn't feel so happy about it. There was a lot going on in my head. And my mouth and face, to be fair.

I don't like the taste of sperm. I know there is a whole 'does she swallow?' thing and women are supposed to swallow and love it. And believe me, I've wanted to swallow and love it. I've tried many times, thinking it would be a nice thing to do for the man I love. But it tastes mank and makes me gag. I remember once when I was little, I was swimming in the cool refreshing sea and I thought how nice it would be to take some refreshing gulps of the cool water. I did so, and proceeded to do an almighty and lengthy burp/gag. It went on for ages as I retched and retched the salty water up. And that is kind of how I feel when I taste sperm. I could maybe dab a bit on my finger and lick it at a push.

So the gag thing was going on in my body, but something else entirely was going on in my head. Because there I was again in a situation that hadn't felt good for me, and I hadn't said anything. I think I felt I couldn't because he was about to ejaculate; we're brainwashed with 'the money shot is king' sex, remember. But actually, I could have stopped and said, 'No, this isn't feeling good for me now.' I'm fairly sure it wouldn't have been the end of the world if his ejaculation had been a bit delayed while we lay down on the floor again.

Looking back, I feel quite a lot of compassion for the situation. I see how hard it was for him to surrender and lend his body to me in this way, and perhaps this was his way of taking back control. Also, I was still so new to being in a leading role when it came to erotic stuff, and incredibly insecure. Hey ho.

Reading material

While my attempts at meeting buddies to explore with weren't going so well, it wasn't by any means a wasted period because this time on my own meant I could focus on my two hobbies: reading and wanking.

Now this was the period when the whole land, and that isn't even a Lucy exaggeration, had gone fully potty over a book that contained quite a lot of the sex. The book was called *Fifty Shades of Grey* and everyone, it seemed, had read it. People I knew who never read anything else had read it, and so had their friends, sisters, mothers and grandmothers. This book reached that surreal tipping point I'd not seen since Dan Brown's *The Da Vinci Code*, where you would go into any bookshop and see full-size bins containing it. 'Have you read *Fifty Shades*?' became a question that absolutely ANYONE might ask you. Eventually it got to the point that I had heard and read so many opinions about it that I felt I had to read it to form my own.

So I read *Fifty Shades of Grey*. But it bothered me, and the phrase 'this is all we need' looped in my brain for quite a while afterwards.

The story centres around a twenty-one-year-old virgin who meets and falls for a rich and troubled businessman. He has his own very well-equipped dungeon and wants her to sign a contract so that he can dominate all aspects of her life. I think the reason this made me sigh and say, 'This is all we need,' so much is that here was I, all excited about directing my own sexual course, and this book seemed, depressingly, to say that women should follow what the men want, much like most porn and most of the other mainstream notions of 'sex' I felt I'd been fed all my life. I wished the story had been about a woman creating her own sexual adventure and deciding what she wanted, not as a response to what a man wanted, but instead because she was really feeling into what she desired.

Maybe I could write that story? I mused. Could I even write my own story?

Another thing about *Fifty Shades* was that it was full of straight-to-penetration sex, which in my experience, and that of most women I've spoken to, is painful. I didn't get turned on reading about it. It made me wince and feel a bit cross.

Perhaps as a response to this, I found myself drawn to writings that depicted sexuality, and in particular female sexuality, as something quite special, sacred even. I felt changed just by reading this stuff.

Living in Brighton I would often grab a cuppa and sit reading on the pebbly beach. I loved the pebbly beach. I'd moved here from London and enjoyed being able to sit somewhere and see so much sky. I felt rocked like a baby by the sound of the waves and would sit and ponder life while fondling pebbles. I took myself to the beach when I was feeling sad or angry and whenever I could I liked to be there as the sun came down.

One evening I was there on the beach with my cup of tea, engrossed in a book about female sexuality. This one was quite esoteric, more so than most I had read, but I was gobbling it up. It took you on a tour of a woman's body, with writings and meditations activating a pathway of sexual energy, which the book referred to as Shakti. It contained an exercise where you had to lie back and focus on and talk to your cervix.

'I'll just lie back and have a wee word with my cervix,' I thought.

I did the meditation, and found that very quickly I had begun to cry. I had the oddest sensation that my body was conveying something to me about an abortion I had had in my early twenties. It wasn't telling me that morally I had been wrong to do what I had done. No, it was more trying to say that the procedure had been very invasive, cold and unpleasant. It was as though my cervix was speaking to me. I lay there crying. I hadn't thought about this abortion for ages and never before in this way. One minute I was bobbing about on the beach with a book and a cuppa, the next I found myself blubbing and floored. I really did cry. It took me quite some time to gather myself and leave the beach that evening. But I didn't mind. In fact, I felt glad of the experience. I remember thinking, 'Of course, I needed to cry like that and let that go, and, of course, it was a horrible, cold procedure that my body didn't enjoy.'

'I like your bell tent'

Then, as if by magic, someone put a festival down the road from me. It wasn't your usual festival full of crowd-surfing and pear cider. This one was just 150 people, no booze at all, a scattering of workshops and acoustic music and poetry in the evenings. I saw that a 'full-body-orgasm workshop' was offered on the programme and, quick as you can say 'massage my base chakra', I purchased a ticket.

I pitched my tent, along with a friend of mine, near a pretty tree in the corner of the camping field. A friendly looking fella in a purple ensemble came by to say hello; he talked about birds and flower remedies, a tall, modern-day elf. Another chap arrived in our little corner and proceeded to unroll a big and rather impressive bell tent. It turned out he knew my friend. The four of us chattered as we scurried about setting up our camps.

I was quite new to camping and festivals. I wrestled with poles while muttering about needing a mallet and having a hole in one of my wellies.

'I have a mallet you could borrow,' Bell Tent Man offered.

'Ooo, marvellous!' I skipped over to take it from him. He had a big smiley stubbly round face. Smiley and stubbly, my favourite combo. Just looking at him made me grin. He wasn't much taller than me, something I took note of as a psychic had once told me that there was a man for me who wasn't much taller than I was. 'Thank you very much. You're very organised!'

He smiled again.

I smiled.

He smiled.

There was a lot of smiling going on.

'That's a very nice big tent you have there,' I said.

'Yes, it's new.'

'It's lovely. I'm not a bit jealous. Thank you kindly for the mallet.' Was I sounding a bit giddy?

'Pleasure.'

I wandered over to my friend.

'How do you know Bell Tent Man?'

'We met at a tantra festival.'

Interesting!

The four of us tent buddies sat down and, after waiting for about thirty-six hours for my friend's camping stove to boil, we had a cup of tea together while I tried really hard not to eat all Bell Tent Man's salt and vinegar crisps.

'I love salt and vinegar crisps,' I offered by way of explanation.

'Lucy wants to write a book about sex,' my friend announced.

I winced. Bell Tent Man smiled.

'Er, yes, about my disastrous search for better nooky, which has taught me more about myself than anything I've ever done before. And which led me to feminism. Which I'm a bit of a fan of.'

'Interesting,' he smiled.

'Yes, but very early stages. Embryonic, in fact. Really only at the stage of telling your friend in confidence.'

'She started the No More Page 3 campaign,' my friend added.

'Wow,' he said. 'I read about that. Caroline Lucas supports it, doesn't she? She wore one of those T-shirts in the Commons.'

I nodded.

'Lucy wears that T-shirt quite a lot at the moment too,' my friend chuckled. 'How's your training going?' she asked Bell Tent Man.

'I've not started yet,' he told her.

'What's the training for?'

'Sexological bodywork.'

Absolutely no idea. None at all. But it did have the word sex in it. So my ears pricked up. I nodded as though I understood and made a mental note to look it up later. I obviously have one of those faces where you can read every thought because he instantly explained what it is.

'It's to become a sex educator. To help people with their erotic development, or with any issues they might have in that area.'

'Is that an actual thing?' I cried. 'Can you sort out my erotic potential and help me ejaculate and be less terrified of a penis?!'

Definitely giddy and oversharing . . .

Public nakedness

The conversation moved on while I drifted off, getting excited about the possibilities that could manifest from meeting a groovy sex doctor. When I did eventually rejoin the conversation the rest of them had decided to check out the sauna.

'Oh, bugger, a sauna, that'll be another blooming "clothing optional space",' I thought to myself. My limited experience of clothing optional spaces had taught me that everyone takes the option to not wear any clothes.

As I had been getting more and more into and confident (ish) with sex, I had been making more friends who were likewise curious about and interested in sex. As a rule, these new friends tended to be really cool and blasé about getting naked in front of each other.

This was still very new territory for me. I used to be utterly and completely petrified of public nakedness. Blimey, it wasn't even that long before I set off on my sex adventure that I was doing some book research at a retreat centre in California, at a place which had these wonderful hot sulphur spring baths, where you could lie on the side of the cliff in a natural stone bath in healing waters, basking in the sun or looking up at the brightest stars you've ever seen. It was amazing. Truly amazing. The one ickle 'but' was that these baths were 'clothing optional'. That's right. So everyone who went to these baths was naked. NAKED! No clothes. And not just that, they were REALLY comfortable about it. They didn't wear their towels around them until they were practically in the baths, and then do a quick 'whip the towel off, submerge body in water' manoeuvre. No, they were all 'saunter into the area waving at people, have whole conversations while standing around with one foot resting on a highish wall, do a spot of yoga' before getting in the baths, oh and after they would hang about in the showers for ages doing a bit of absent-minded chi gong. Yep, they were naked around other people LIKE THIS WAS NO BIG DEAL!

It was a nightmare. People I met who were really nice, and who I loved hanging out with would say, 'We're going to the baths later, do you want to come?' as naturally as if they were inviting me to the pub. And I would be screaming 'noooooooooooooooooooooo!!!!!' inside, thinking of an excuse while trying to act nonchalant. The only time I would go to the baths would be when I thought no one else, or hardly anyone else, would be there.

It was such a shame: there I was, in one of THE most beautiful places on earth, panicking about showing my uncovered body to people.

One night a naked didgeridoo meditation was being held in the baths. I'll repeat that, a NAKED DIDGERIDOO MEDITATION, where everyone, including the didgeridoo player, would be naked. I couldn't pass up the opportunity to go to a naked didgeridoo meditation, it would be foolish. This was terrific book research. I had to bloomin' well go along.

Crikey, did I freak out beforehand. I panted with fear. I burst into tears. In the end, I had to be escorted there by a woman I was sharing a room with and hugged for fifteen minutes before I found the strength to enter in my towel and do the speedy 'edge of the bath, whip towel off and dunk'. Others there were enjoying sensual massages and allowing the didgeridoo to vibrate all over their exposed flesh. They quivered and moaned while I sat up to my neck in water in the darkest corner I could find, making sure I wasn't touching anyone else.

But on this day at the festival with Bell Tent Man and the others I thought, 'The more I do this the easier it will feel.' So I got naked and had a sauna. There were no histrionics at all. A little bit of shyness, and a few little thoughts bubbled about the size of my bottom, but I managed to nudge them away. The scene of sensual freedom was slightly marred by the fact that the sauna hadn't warmed up yet, but you can't have everything.

As we tucked into some vegan cheesecake afterwards (it was vegan lasagne for dinner) I felt a teensy bit proud of myself. I was quite drawn to Bell Tent Man; he felt like a kindred spirit, and there we were about an hour after the first introduction and he already knew I was a feminist on a sex mission and had seen me naked. I liked the honesty and openness of it all. Later that night he swapped one of his wellies for my leaky one and asked me if I wanted to partner him at the full-body-orgasm workshop the next day.

Full-body orgasm

I'd put 'full-body orgasm' on my list of sexy wants without knowing too much about what it entailed. Understandably, I'd heard the term and thought, 'Full-body orgasm, yes, please, where do I sign up?' An orgasm is a pleasurable experience, so one that can span your entire body must surely be Pleasure MAX. Pleasure Fusion Power. Pleasure Mach3 Turbo. Now I'm using Gillette razor names and saying them in my head in a deep male cinema advert voice. Perhaps I've been at the computer too long today.

Anyhoo, you get the picture, I was (understandably) excited about experiencing the full-body orgasm.

I attended the workshop, but sadly there was no orgasming for me, either full-bodied or localised. Possibly because I was in a massive hall full of other people valiantly giving the full-body orgasm a go too, and all the letting go and channelling energy stuff can be a bit tricky with seventy strangers in the room.

There was a demonstration to start with. The crowd in the room sat on the floor, legs crossed or out in front, a bit like school assembly when you are eight, except for the partially clothed hippy on the floor. Another woman started waving her arms over this woman on the floor, and the woman on the floor began to moan, groan and writhe. Then we were told to have a go. But despite being partnered with Bell Tent Man, nothing really happened for me. I just lay there, listening to the couple next to me having an argument about who was going to go first. I left the workshop baffled rather than quivering.

Afterwards Bell Tent Man and I hung out. We bobbed around the festival, chatted by the open fire, walked in the woods, and were then reborn in a teepee. As you do. The rebirthing workshop involved lying on a crowded floor doing a LOT of quick deep breathing. This was hardcore breathing. It made the panting at the tantra workshop look like Igglepiggle in *In the Night Garden*. I went for it until my body was almost spasming. I drooled and snotted and cried with Bell Tent Man next to me. Afterwards I felt clear and high.

We went back to his bell tent and shared an apple. Never has there been such a delicious apple.

'At the end of this apple, I am going to ask him if he would like to kiss,' I thought. It seemed like the most obvious thing in the world and very stress-free for me.

But before I had finished the apple we did that thing where you smile at each other for ages and it just naturally becomes a kiss.

'What would you like to do?' he asked after quite a lot of passionate snogging.

I thought about it.

'Shall we get naked, go very slowly and see what happens?' I suggested.

He nodded. Check me out, I've turned into Naked Lu.

We spent the next few hours kissing, caressing and having incredibly slow, intense sex. I loved how much better I knew my body from all the wanking, and how much easier I found it to surrender to big orgasms.

'Tell me when you would like me to come,' he said at one point.

Well, I'd never heard this before. Was he really giving me the power to grant his orgasm?! Blimey, I was to be the decision maker, and I had always been dreadful at making decisions.

We lay there afterwards, chatting for hours.

At one point he mentioned that he hadn't been in a monogamous relationship for a few years.

'Interesting,' I murmured.

I told him about my experience with the Dark-Haired German man and how the more open relationship had suited me.

The next morning my friend and I had a catch-up about the festival. Very quickly we got on to Bell Tent Man.

'What do you think about us getting together?' I asked.

'Well, he's a tantra bloke. He'll be very good in bed. Very practised. Enjoy that. But don't fall in love with him.'

I nodded. 'Don't fall in love with him,' I repeated for good measure. Simples. As if.

Bell Tent Man and I proceeded to spend pretty much the whole festival together. Being with a fella had never felt so effortless. It was so bloomin' effortless that I didn't think about it at all until the end of the weekend when I remembered that we lived hours apart.

'What do we do?' I said, lying post-coitally on a lilo before we had to go.

'I don't know,' he smiled.

'Well, I do have an idea! We could make a list of sexual things we would like to do and explore together and meet up and do them.'

'It's a deal.'

A new list

And so I made another list of things I wanted to do with Bell Tent Man and sent it to him.

1. Spend a whole day in bed, making love, snoozing, listening to folk music, possibly watching a movie or a few episodes of an American serialised drama

2. Go to a sex party in nature . . .

I have no fixed fantasies or expectations about this. I would like to follow the feelings, and explore my wildness if it arises!! *(This one surprised me, to be honest!)*

3. Explore something with a woman

This is something I've been curious about for a while. I think because I adore my own sensuality and know how to pleasure myself, I am drawn to the idea of lovingly touching a woman and bringing her to orgasm. It is something I could imagine doing with you, i.e. the two of us giving pleasure to another woman, and myself and another woman lovingly and playfully pleasuring you.

4. I would like some time with your body!!!

To really explore where and how you like to be touched. Especially your penis. I'd like to offer you a lovely lingam massage. Although be warned, I have a bit of a hang-up around this!

5. I have never properly masturbated in front of someone and I think I would like to, even though the thought does make me feel slightly exposed/vulnerable, but in a tender way

I think it could be a lovely thing to share. I'd love to see you touch yourself and to feel my arousal and explore that on my body.

6. BDSM

I have no kinky experience but would like to dip my toe in a bit to see what all the fuss is about.

7. Make some porn

This is more one for me to do on my own. It's all very well for me to criticise it, but what sort of porn would I make if I gave myself the chance? It also strikes me that making porn is something more women should have a bash at. If we leave the porn-making to the men, well, then, we are basically letting them represent, or own, sex. Maybe that is quite a dramatic statement but I do think there's truth there. If we even up the output might that change things, and if so, how . . .? Ooo, exciting!

'Wow,' I thought as I sent this message, 'I have come a long way.'

On the table

The first thing we decided to do was an exchange. I would give Bell Tent Man one of my world-famous lingam massages and he would give me a yoni massage. The yoni massage came first.

Now, previously, incidents of hands other than my own going on or in my pubic region had occurred either because something was wrong down there, i.e. someone from the medical profession was having a gander, or because sex was on the cards. The only time it was an end in itself was back in the days of 'fingering'. And I thank the Lord that the tantric yoni massages I received bore no resemblance to my memories of being fingered. Imagine a normal massage that includes your vulva and vagina, and you'll have the idea. Although not a massage like a pal of mine received in Nepal, where the masseuse was also having a conversation on her mobile phone. Think more of the kind of massage that you might get at a spa, say, which has an element of ritual to it, or worship even, where you feel you are being pampered.

Bell Tent Man could actually do massage, he'd done courses and everything, and he had his own massage table. I went to his place and he had set up said massage table in a toasty room, with, wait for it, an open fire. He had lit candles, warmed oil and Ludovico Einaudi was playing. I felt a bit emotional just entering the room and seeing that he had done all this for me.

I lay down naked. Faint thoughts of women sacrificed on tables swirled in my head. But then there were firm, kind hands on my head, my shoulders, running down my arms and back, all the way down to my feet. I felt myself letting go of all the little weights I hadn't even realised I'd been carrying. Firm hands on my shoulders made me groan, as they did when they kneaded my feet. My body was now rolling and moving in response to his touch. I was being softened, made malleable. It felt sublime. Every time a new area was released I sighed or groaned.

Yoni massage

Make sure you (the yoni massage giver) are relaxed. A massage from someone who is stressed and worried about missing *Enders* is not a calming experience. Take some time to be still beforehand. Sit quietly and focus on your breathing, do a short mediation or mindfulness practice (there is lots of this sort of stuff on YouTube if you are new to it) or have a bath, listen to relaxing music, that type of thing.

You ideally want to earmark an hour and a half for this.

Set up the space: relaxing music, candles, tidy bed, etc.

You will need lots of oil! Coconut is great.

Welcome the person with the yoni into your comfortable space.

Sit for a few moments together and look into each other's eyes. No need to speak, just take some deep breaths together.

Ask the person with a yoni to please take off their clothes and lie down on their tummy.

Before you make contact with their body, take a moment to connect with your own hands. You are offering a loving and healing experience with these hands; this person is precious, touch them as such.

Start with gentle, loving, sweeping strokes up and down the whole body to awaken it. Then move to the feet, before kneading and stroking up the legs, then to the hands and up the arms, then down the back and over the bottom.

Do the same on the other side.

Start to incorporate long strokes over her pubic area and in between her legs. Start gently, increasing pressure, cupping your hand over the pubic area, opening out the fingers so they run over the lips and clitoris. Massage the lips, squeeze them together, keeping the movements rhythmic if you can. Then, making sure the hands are very well oiled, gently part the lips and explore the vulva in slow strokes, building in speed, being careful not to touch the clitoris directly. Keep the fingers moving either side of it and around; some recommend tracing the alphabet with your finger around the clitoris.

Very slowly and gently insert a lubricated middle finger into the yoni. Move the finger in tiny rhythmic circular motions, covering as much of the vagina as you are able to. Ask the person receiving, in a soothing voice, how the touch feels to them. Keep checking in and remind them to breathe if necessary. Remember the idea here is not to chase an orgasm. One might come – if so, welcome it – but don't go chasing.

Finish off by some relaxing strokes across the whole body. The receiver might just want to be on their own for

a while, or to snuggle up. Check what they want and try
to keep everything relaxed afterwards.

I rolled onto my back. My face and neck were stroked and
squeezed, and then my hands, breasts, and legs. I opened my legs
so that my thighs could be pushed and pressed. His touch worked
its way to my labia. More oil. Little strokes and pinches mingled
with longer caresses. The area around my clitoris was included.
Then the entrance to my vagina. I was aware of fingers touching
me internally. It wasn't necessarily always pleasant. Sometimes I
made sounds of pain or discomfort, and more often than not the
pain would yield with more touch. 'Breathe,' he would remind
me. At one point, the touch felt uncomfortable, so I took a big
inhale. The sensation deepened. It felt jagged, stark, and a wave
of emotion came over me that I was unable to protect myself
from. Before I could catch it, I found I was sobbing.

'Breathe,' he said, gently. His fingers stayed where they
were but the pressure relaxed. Oh my goodness, I suddenly felt
exhausted, as though I'd been holding something really heavy
and horrid for ages and I had just finally been able to let it go. It
was as though I was crying for some great tragedy, and I couldn't
quite place my finger on what it was. Wow, there was so much
emotional pain there. I cried for quite a while. I forgot all about
Bell Tent Man until I started to come through the other side.

'How are you doing?' he smiled kindly. 'Do you want to
carry on?'

I nodded.

He started the internal massage again, ever so gently. I did
my best to breathe. I felt vulnerable after my outburst. Exposed.
'Like an egg without a shell,' as my friend says. But, perhaps
weirdly, that was OK. I felt safe with Bell Tent Man and this
experience.

Then, suddenly, I crashed into another wall of emotion.

Fuckadoodle. What was going on here? I was mega-crying now. Yowling in fact.

'Breathe,' he encouraged me.

I was taken back again to the abortion I had in my early twenties. I found myself apologising to the girl, I felt sure it had been a girl, for not being able to keep her.

I couldn't carry on with the session after that, and I couldn't speak for a long while. It all seemed so strange, so 'out there' or 'woo woo'. He wrapped me in a blanket. I lay there until I felt able to get up and speak.

'When I went like that . . . what had you been doing?' I asked eventually.

'I was touching your cervix,' he told me simply.

Bell Tent Man and I did more of this sort of touch over the next few months, sometimes structured like this, sometimes during lovemaking, and I cried a lot. Often it felt like I was crying for the way I'd experienced sex over the years. Sometimes particular sexual situations or relationships that I hadn't thought about for years would drift into my mind. Sometimes it wouldn't be one isolated experience that came to me, but a sense of the weight of many. It feels odd confessing this, and it's quite hard to explain, but each time I cried in this way, I appreciated the release it gave me. I felt better, clearer, stronger afterwards, and more in tune with myself.

Once areas have been traumatised they go numb to stop it happening again. Touching them consciously and gently reactivates them. People who do sexual healing call it de-armouring. Before I learned this I simply called it tenderness. I think tender touch has a huge capacity to heal, and so often we women have a lot to heal in this area.

MEN'S BITS

'Gahhhh! It's a penis!' – Me

Oh penises! Penises! Penises! I'd long been terrified of the penis, in the 'excited/TERRIFIED' sense of the word.

My problem was still that I wasn't sure what to do with these penises. They grew, they morphed, they exploded (or not), and I had no confidence in how I was supposed to facilitate this journey for them. Remember the thumb and finger ace sign on the grassy knoll? Well, I hadn't really got much beyond it. I did know that they (well, one at a time generally) could go in my vagina, which was something, I suppose. But actually that fact meant that quite often in the past I'd allowed penetrative sex before I was really ready. It was a safer way to take care of the penis than it being in my hand or mouth. If only I had said, 'Can I practise some moves on your penis, please?' to the boys when we were teenagers, we could have had a fun and educational afternoon or two. But as I've mentioned, I couldn't really talk honestly and openly to people with penises and I was utterly petrified of rejection.

The outcome of all this was that I was a woman in my thirties and I was still winging it with a penis. I needed more uninterrupted time with a willy to learn and practise a few moves for my toolkit. I had tried this before, of course, but my previous attempts included the dire attempt while holding a book, drunk, the one where I laughed as he ejaculated, and the one with the Transit van.

Lingam massage #4: CUPCAKES AND BUNTING! SHE'S A SEX GODDESS!!

Lucy Does Lingam Massage Take Number Four was a goodie, but before we launch the 'And aaaaaction', I had best fill you in about some goings on.

Bell Tent Man and I had started to meet up regularly despite the long distance between us. Sometimes we would meet up to do things on the list, but more often than not we would just meet up to make, and hang, out with each other. It soon became apparent, to me at least, that something was going on. You see, when we were together it was, well, I know I said it before, but it was just so effortless and easy to be together, and the sex was reeeeeally gooooood. I once timed one of our 'quickies'. It was thirty-seven minutes.

The only problem in all this was that when we weren't together I was all over the place. I was a liability. I left my phone in the far-away city he lived in twice. I had to cancel a meeting once because I had arrived at the train station and had left my wallet at home. I rescheduled, and made it into London, only to realise I had the wrong day. Then there was the time when I purchased a train ticket to take me to a speaking engagement, but the train was set to arrive while I was supposed to be speaking. I mean, you can probably tell from the nature of this book that I have a capacity for chaos, but even by my standards the first weeks and months of getting to know Bell Tent Man had me flailing around like an unattended toddler in an antique-porcelain showroom. We might have started out all cool and busy and open, but it was looking like we could be . . . you know . . . falling in . . . dare I say it . . . LOVE. (Cue dramatic music – dun, dun, duuuun!)

Anyhoo, back to the lingam massage: I intended to lie him down, make his whole body feel amazing and then top it off with a lovely posh handjob. What I didn't want to do was get cross, panicky or fall down some hysterical pit of self-consciousness.

I went to town this time.

Here's what I did.

1. I created an alter ego

Yeah, it surprised me a bit too this one, but I found myself saying, 'Do you mind if I pretend I'm a newly qualified professional masseuse who is a bit crap at massage, and we don't know each other?'

Caught a bit off guard, he agreed.

2. I set up the ritualistic spa space

The lingam massage articles emphasised 'setting the scene' each time. You couldn't just mute the timber-clad-home episode of *Grand Designs* and say, 'Get your cock out.' You both had to be relaxed and not worrying about the grill being on.

I ran a candlelit bath with bubbles, popped him in it, and said, 'I'll be back in twelve minutes with a warm towel.' Then I set up the room with more candles and played another 'sensual massage' playlist from Spotify. I even sat down and meditated a bit before the twelve minutes was up.

3. I started well

'I am new to doing lingam massage,' I said as my 'I don't know you' alter ego, holding his hands and looking into his eyes. 'But I promise to honour your body with my love and attention.' Wahoo, I was rocking this!

4. I massaged him all over first (and managed not to get humphy)

The all-over body massage is supposed to awaken the sensitivity of his whole body so that energy can flow all over him and heighten his pleasure. I guess it's why sex is so good after exercise, or swimming in the sea on holiday: your body is just more alive to touch, sensation and orgasm.

I massaged his back first and then turned him over onto his front, slowly working my way to the top of his thighs. I played with pressure; sometimes I was kneading, sometimes using little feather strokes. He was getting a bit 'sigh-y' as I slowly worked my way upwards, surrendering to what I was doing. When he made sounds and sighs because it was feeling particularly good, it gave me confidence.

I let go of expectation and followed my instincts. I loved simply seeing where I wanted to touch him. I tuned out all the chatter in my head, so that I was almost dancing with his body. As with most things, I found that if I thought about it too much it turned to shit, whereas if I followed the feeling it could be rather magical.

5. I massaged his perineum, balls and then moved on to his penis
I busted out the moves I'd learned on Google, introducing each one as I went.

'Are you all right there? I'm just going to pull my hand upward in a traditional wanker-sign grip,' I said. And, 'now for the pulling downward in a traditional wanker-sign grip'.

Other moves were:

- The 'start the fire' one, where you hold your hands as though you're just about to clap, pop the penis in between the hands and rub back and forth up and down the shaft (that one went down very well, I could literally feel his energy building there).
- Another move where you sort of slap the tip back and forth with one hand; I had a bash but not sure that one really worked.
- I 'juiced' the tip and also massaged it gently.

- I built energy with the penis, went back to the balls and perineum for a bit and then quickly made some long strokes across his whole body. I did that a few times. I'd read somewhere that if you can build an orgasm to a near peak six times, when you do actually come it will be fan-bloomin'-tastic.

And that was pretty much it. It went down very very well. I thoroughly recommend.

Becoming a penis geek

Now, that I was hanging out regularly with a penis I thought I had better swot up a bit. So, as is my wont, I took to the internet and I found that doing searches to find out about the sensitive parts of the penis was FASCINATING! I wish I had done this aeons ago, because it made me feel far more empowered, confident and keen to be around the little fellas.

'Can I just borrow your penis for a few minutes?' I would ask Bell Tent Man.

'But I'm watching James Bond.'

'I won't be long, I just want to check it against this great penis diagram on my computer.'

'Ooookaay.'

'Will you take your jeans and pants off?'

'All right.' He did so. 'I feel like a toddler on a beach.'

Me squinting at the computer and then back to the penis on the sofa. 'Ooo.'

'What?'

'Ooo, look at that!'

'What?' He sounded a bit alarmed.

Me, very excitedly, 'Well, I read that light touches on your foreskin here could give you an erection. And look, he's erect!'

'Mmm, that's pretty much the best way to get it erect.'

I sighed. 'It's like I am a sex genius.'

This is what I discovered.

The sensitive hotspots are:

Glans – the smooth shiny bulbous end bit of the penis is often said to be the most sensitive area.

Foreskin/prepuce – this is the retractable double layer of skin that covers the glans (tip of the penis). Some argue that *this* piece of skin, especially the rim of it, is the most sensitive area of the penis. It has an inner and outer layer. The outer layer, as I mentioned above, often likes gentle touch, which can trigger an erection. The inner layer is rich in sensory nerve endings and erogenous tissue. It appears to be all about the foreskin! You can well see how that sensitive inner layer of the foreskin would like to be rubbed against the sensitive glans.

The coronal ridge/corona – this is the rim of tissue that divides the main shaft of the penis from the glans at the top. Interesting name for a beer.

Frenulum/frenum – this is the web-like bit of tissue that attaches the foreskin to the glans. For some it can be, to quote the awesome Scarleteen website, 'the most intensely sensitive part of the whole penis'.[1] In fact, there is a chap online who demonstrates giving himself a 'fremgasm' by tapping and stimulating the frenulum on his erect penis with just the tip of his finger.

Frenular delta – this is the triangular bit of the frenulum under the coronal ridge. Pull the foreskin back and tap here!

The perineal raphe – this is the rather cool dividing line or seam you can see that goes along the underside of the penis, down the middle of the scrotum and towards the anus.

The scrotum/scrotal sac – this is the thin baggy bit of skin which houses the testicles or balls. Sensitive to touch.

Testicles/balls – the two small bags that make sperm and hormones.

Perineum – this firm patch of skin between the scrotum and the anus is actually an erogenous zone. Apparently, it likes firm touch as this is how you can stimulate the prostate indirectly without entering the anus. Oh, internet research, I love you. I'd always been confused as to what the fabled perineum was all about.

Prostate – the male prostate is the equivalent to the female G-spot and it is found a few inches up the fella's bum on the belly side. It is a pretty big deal, with more nerve endings than the penis.

Now, I'm talking about foreskins here but obviously not all men have them (because somehow there is still a belief that it is ok to cut a bit of baby's willy off) and I am told that these circumsized penises like to be touched with a lot of oil.

Learning all this made me want to scoop out a job lot of the old coconut oil and lightly touch all these bits and bobs of the penis. Penis bobs. I rather like that name.

'Can I just have a quick look at your frenulum?' I would say.

'What? Now?'

'Is that OK? I'll get you erect first.'

Fumble. Fiddle.

'What's that you are doing?'

'Trying to give you a fremgasm.'

'A what?'

'I really want to give you a fremgasm.'

'Lucy, are you all right?'

Up the bum!

As I said, the fella's equivalent to a G-spot is called a prostate and is found about two to three inches up his bum on the belly side. Bell Tent Man allowed me to find his. Yikes. Brave man.

Back in the day, whenever the day was, I remember hearing almost mythical stories of how some women, I think particularly French women, would pop their fingers up a fella's bottie during intercourse and have him exploding with delight. In my head thereafter the Frenchies were the bona fide sex champions of the world.

But let's just take a moment here to PANIC. If I had been terrified by my lack of confidence and prowess with the penis, then I was quivering under the table screeching for Mummy at the thought of trying to give pleasure to someone by finding something I couldn't see, in a place I'd never been. It wasn't all boding terribly well in this area then.

I didn't want to extemporise sticking my finger up Bell Tent Man's arse. I wanted to do more of a relaxing massage-y thing before exploring up the bum. Thankfully, 'relaxing, massage-y, exploring the up-the-bum thing' has a name. Hurrah! Prostate massage. I thought I'd have a go at that.

As ever, I set to work doing some research. I ended up involved in a few Reddit threads to see what people were saying about anal play. These conversations veered from guys saying they LOVED doing anal play themselves, or their partners COULDN'T GET ENOUGH of their anuses, to guys saying they thought that anal play was the most disgusting thing in the world, or their partners thought it was the most disgusting thing in the world, or, very often, they *thought* that their partners would think it was the most disgusting thing in the world. Gay men seemed quite at home talking about anal play, while straight men were all over the shop with the issue.

I found articles online written by doctors detailing the health benefits of prostate massage. And there was lots of info on YouTube about how to give a prostate massage, including a woman on a US TV chat show demonstrating how to do it with a walnut inside a partially blown-up condom. And there's a book called *Anal Pleasure and Health* by a man called Jack Morin, which, as you might have guessed, is all about getting to know this area in order to heal and explore its pleasure.

Research about how to do any anal play stressed three things: cut your fingernails, go slow, reeeeally slow, and use LOADS, and I mean LOADS, of lube, because the anal canal doesn't lubricate itself like the vagina. I attended a wonderful 'how to give a great blowjob' workshop at the women's sex shop Sh!, and the hilarious women who led it talked about touching the prostate for his pleasure. Their two big rules were 1) CONSENT – don't just pop a finger up there, ask first!! And 2) Yes, LUBE!

Now, I can't help but feel that my online porn sex education had majorly failed me here, because I don't remember EVER having seen lube used in porn. I'll say that again in case you were dozing off: I DON'T REMEMBER HAVING EVER SEEN LUBRICANT USED BEFORE ANAL PENETRATION IN PORN! I find this fact really crap.

Anyhoo. Let's crack on. So to speak.

The logistics of doing a prostate massage are pretty much the same as when giving a lingam massage: create a soothing environment and then massage him until he is relaxed, paying particular attention to the buttocks and upper thighs. Then gently touch the area around the anus, gradually moving towards the anus itself, building the pressure as you feel appropriate. Keep everything very lubricated, and, making sure nothing is uncomfortable, press and stroke firmly on and around the hole, and start to very gently but firmly push with the tip of your finger inside. OK, we need to talk about fingernails here. I would not try this with fake nails on! You ideally want short nails filed smooth for this. I did hear (again, by the wonderful women at Sh! Have I mentioned how warm, hilarious and unashamed they are about sex?) that some women keep their nails long but use plastic gloves and stuff cotton wool in the fingers of those gloves before putting them on.

So you are gently but firmly pushing your finger inside the anus. But again, only if it is comfortable for the guy – keep talking through it. It definitely shouldn't be in any way painful and it won't work at all if either or both of you are tense. We tried a few times and didn't get to the prostate; we just had a few anal massages to start with to get used to the whole thing. But what can happen when you press your finger in a bit, if everyone is relaxed, is kinda weird and very cool, because the bum hole then sort of leads the way itself. If it is relaxed enough it doesn't just let you in, it sort of pulls you in of its own accord, in a 'whoa, this is spooky, my finger is being pulled up your arse' sort of way. From there you can start to find and gently touch the prostate.

A couple of inches up the back passage, you will come across a bump which feels slightly rougher than the smooth canal you have travelled up. You might only just reach it with the tip of your finger; go for gentle but firm come-hither strokes, as opposed to little fingertip tickles, on and around this area.

If you are worried about cleanliness you could buy some latex gloves; you can get them online quite cheaply, and there is something quite fun and kinky about being in a carnal tryst while wearing the hand attire of the cold-meat counter. Or he might prefer to use an anal douche, a little plastic squeezy thing that you use to squirt water up your bum to clean it beforehand. If you don't want to go up there with your finger itself, you can also buy a prostate massager, or pop some anal beads up there. (Anal beads are nice soft little rubbery beads.)

BUT WHATEVER YOU DO – DON'T FORGET THE LUBE!*

Quick blowjob tip

One thing I did learn at the 'how to give a great blowjob' workshop at the mega-lovely female sex shop Sh! in London is a great blowjob tip! When you bear down onto the cock/pecker/willy, inhale, and when you draw your head up again, exhale. Seriously, try it. Revolutionary.

---

*Lube! Did I mention the lube?

THE SUMMER OF SEX

The sex festival

What followed was a veritable summer of sexy love spent largely in a certain person's bell tent.

It was kicked off by going to the summer Conscious Sexuality Festival in Dorset. Yes, yes, you did read that right. I, Lucy-Anne Holmes, went to a sex festival. And I loved it.

Well, not at first. I absolutely hated it when I arrived. Two hundred and fifty people. Most in brightly coloured organic fabrics. All shiny-eyed and smiling, giving each other thirty-second hugs. I wasn't comfortable at all. That first night, there was a lot of 'checking each other out' going on. You'd be talking to someone, but that person would be constantly distracted, say by a fine bottom in leggings, or by someone they particularly gelled with while doing some cathartic movement the year before. I didn't like the atmosphere at all. It felt like everyone was somewhere else. The food was nice, though.

After the first dinner, we all had to gather in a marquee where loud music was playing. Most people arrived and instantly started dancing and jumping around. I stood there, wincing and humphing. 'Why did I want to go on this sodding sexual adventure? I should be polishing off a bottle of Pinot Grigio somewhere like a normal person.' It was all a bit much. Bell Tent Man was bopping about with the rest of them, gleefully being reunited with people he already knew. I spotted a fella who was also clinging to the edge of the marquee.

'Have you been before?' I shouted.

'No.'

'Me neither. Not sure I'm into it.'

He shook his head, panic in his eyes. I nodded in agreement and turned back to the crowd. I noticed that a young woman had taken her top off and was dancing wildly with her breasts on display. She looked so comfortable and free. She made it seem odd that people should be wearing clothes at all. 'Oh crikey, what have I done? I am so not ready for this,' I thought, and escaped to my car. I sat inside with the doors locked, then went on Facebook and sent out a virtual scream for help.

When I returned to the marquee things had calmed down a little; the music had stopped and the teachers were introducing themselves and their work. A tanned and charismatic man gave a welcome speech.

'Now, as we're in Britain and there are a lot of English people here,' he said, 'I just want to say that you're bound to be fine, and nothing will come up for you or trigger you.'

Everyone laughed. It was good to know that we were probably all a bit fucked-up when it came to sex. There were a few dos and don'ts and we were wished a wonderful week. I started to relax and even feel excited. I looked at the packed programme, and while some of it seemed WAY over my head – Kink evening! Clothing-optional candlelit ecstatic dance party! YIKES! – lots and lots of it intrigued me, especially as there were so many female teachers. I even found myself skipping along to the sauna afterwards.

It was like being at sex school

I went to my first workshop the next morning. It was led by a very experienced tantra teacher called Jan Day and her partner Frieder. She introduced herself, explaining that she helped people to open up to a celebration of sexuality, but that doing this 'is not safe unless people are able to say no', so we would be doing quite a lot of practice around tuning in to ourselves, asking for what we wanted, and giving and receiving nos.

'Ha, this is awesome!' I thought. These were all the bits I'd been struggling alone with for months.

The focus at the start was on this 'tuning in' to ourselves. We sat down, closed our eyes and then took a few deeper than usual breaths, turning our attention inside and noticing what, and how, we were feeling. I loved this. It reminded me of my German friends and their check-ins and 'how are you feeling in your body?' comments. When I tuned into myself that day I felt fluttery and excited.

The next exercise had us standing opposite our partners, at quite a distance away from them. One person was the mover, the other had to stand still. It was a silent exercise where the standing-still person had two different hand positions to communicate to the other. One was palms up and out flat, as though stopping traffic. The other had the arms down but slightly out from the sides, palms facing the partner in a welcoming gesture. If the standing-still person had their hands in the down gesture then the mover could take one step towards the standing person. If the hands were up, they had to stop. It was a slow exercise. Before each step there was a tuning-in period where each person could close their eyes if necessary and ask themselves, 'Do I want this person to come closer to me? Do I want to come closer to this person?'

Exercise three had us in groups of four. We stood in huddles and each person had a turn in the centre for about ten minutes.

The other people were available to serve that person with their touch. The person in the middle closed their eyes and tuned in to themselves and then said 'zero', 'one', 'two' or 'three', which is how many people they would like to touch them. If they said 'one', one person would start touching them very gently. The person in the middle would then say 'yes', 'no', 'please', 'pause', or 'stop'. 'Yes' was an encouraging, 'I like that.' 'No' was a 'not there' or 'not like that'. With a 'no', the person in the middle had to take hold of the hand that was touching them and either move it or demonstrate the touch they would like. 'Please' was, 'Ooo, I like that a lot. More please!' 'Pause' was, 'I'm not sure about this; just stay as you are but stop what you are doing so I can tune in to myself.' 'Stop' was hands off, everything stops. Before the touch started there was a little check-in point where you could say, 'Please don't touch my face, breasts, or genital area,' or wherever you might not want to be touched, or you could say, 'I don't have any boundaries, but might say stop if that changes.'

I was grouped with two men and one other woman. I think we were all somewhere in our thirties, although one of the guys might have been slightly younger. The two men seemed shy, polite and excited, which might have been how I would have been perceived too, with all my nervous smiles and 'feel free to go first' gestures. Thankfully, the other woman seemed far more relaxed. It emerged she had been to the festival before. Smiley, with curly hair, voluptuous in a pair of shorts and a halterneck top, she stepped into the middle first.

'I am happy for you to touch me anywhere,' she smiled.

She seemed so happy and at ease. 'Wow,' I thought, registering this for a moment. 'I have permission to touch this woman on her face, or her breast; I could put my hand in between her legs.' It seemed almost unbelievable.

Out of the corner of my eye I saw one of Bell Tent Man's friends in another group stand in the middle of his huddle and take all his clothes off. 'Oh my,' I thought, thankful to be where I was.

Very soon we were all gently caressing our new friend, who was giggling and sighing at all the different sensations. I started very gently running my fingers up and down her arms; she let out a little moan when my hand brushed over her breast. So I caressed her breast again.

'Yes,' she said clearly.

I touched her other breast, my fingers causing her nipple to harden under the fabric of her top.

'Please,' she said.

Seeing her enjoying the touch so much enabled me to do the same when it was my go. Like her, I gave no boundaries; then I closed my eyes and very soon was being touched by three pairs of hands. I writhed and moaned under all this touch. I loved it when hands touched my breasts and clitoris area. When it was over I threw my head back and laughed at how much I had enjoyed it.

When the session ended, the other woman from my group turned to me.

'I'm really reminded when I am here how much I like to be touched by and touch women,' she said.

'Same for me. It was really lovely for me too. Thank you,' I replied, and we hugged. One of the long ones. The oxytocin kicks in after twenty seconds of hugging, apparently. I learned that in a cuddle workshop; that's when you start going a bit gooey. We took a few deep breaths in and out as we embraced before saying cheerio.

At lunchtime, I gaily told Bell Tent Man that I wanted to come back every year. It seemed like such a lovely way to get in touch with my sexuality and sensuality.

'I'm feeling great. All stroked and sauna-ed and I haven't even been here for twenty-four hours.'

But I suddenly stopped talking when I overheard a woman, sitting on the grass nearby, calling out to a man.

'Would you like to caress my breasts?' she said. I was sure that was what she had said.

'Oh, well, I was about to go and call my mum, but um, yes, that would be rather nice.'

When I looked, because obviously I had to look, she had a man either side of her, stroking her bare breasts.

'Wow,' I whispered.

I loved having my breasts caressed. I couldn't believe how she had just asked for something like that. It seemed radical, which is kind of ridiculous if you think about it. How is that I could be so completely inspired by a woman asking for what she wants like this? I guess it's because I don't think I had encountered it before. I couldn't recollect ever having seen or heard something like that from a woman before. Especially not in all my porn watching.

I did more workshops over the coming days. In fact, I never missed an opportunity to do a workshop. It was knackering but brilliant. I felt as though I was developing and exercising new muscles in areas, like communicating my wants and needs, where I had been very weak before.

In another workshop Jan Day said, 'We have to learn that it is totally fine for anyone to want anything, and also that it's totally fine to say no. It's OK to *not* get and it is OK to *not* give. Both are OK.' This was another 'wow' moment for me. I had always thought that someone's want had to be appeased, especially if it was a man's.

I found that I was full marks great at giving enthusiastic consent, saying a big smiley 'yes' when someone I liked offered to gently touch my neck, or kiss me softly. But of course sometimes I didn't want what was being offered, and then I had to find my 'no'. A 'no, thank you, that's going a bit far for me' or 'no, that's going too fast' or 'no, it just doesn't feel right for me'. Or just a simple clear, I don't need to explain myself here, 'No.'

As you can probably imagine, as someone who was a serial snogger of people she didn't necessarily fancy, I needed to practise these nos. I particularly had to work on not allowing things to happen which I wasn't comfortable with because I felt sorry for the other person and didn't want to upset them by giving them a 'no'.

It worked the other way, too. I learned how it felt to hear a 'no' when someone didn't want me close to them. OH MY GOD I'VE BEEN REJECTED – WHERE'S THE HARD LIQUOR? wasn't a response that was suggested if you encountered a 'no' at the summer Conscious Sexuality Festival. 'Thank you for looking after yourself,' was preferred. Rejection was seen as a wonderful way for a person to take care of their own needs, allowing you to trust that whatever happened with that person was whole-hearted.

I had one situation that felt awful at the time. It was during a fifteen-minute session where we took it in turns to ask for what we wanted. 'Can I kiss you?' 'Can I play with your hair?' 'Touch your breast?' Whatever you were feeling. I ended up being partnered with a man, and for some reason I really couldn't put my finger on, I didn't want this chap near me. Everything he asked for I had to say no to. By the end of the twenty minutes I was just about able to have a fully clothed hug with him. I had felt guilty during the session. 'If he was partnered with someone else he could be breast-fondling,' I thought. 'As it is he's with me and I can barely sit next to him.' At the end of the session he said, 'Thank you, I needed that.' Which was great, actually, as so had I. Maybe he had to learn hearing the nos and I had to practise saying them. It marked a shift for me: the old Lucy would have let him come too close; she would have felt too guilty saying no.

Finding and expressing my own personal boundaries in any situation was something else that was new to me. I had not really come across the word 'boundaries' before the sexy festival. At first, I was resistant to it. I wanted to live without boundaries. I didn't want to create a prison for myself or anyone else. But then again, if I imagined doing an exercise and someone putting their finger up my bum, I could well see the benefit of having established my boundaries beforehand.

I had a feeling that if I had been to this festival before I asked the man with the nice eyes if he wanted to get together for some tantra, I don't think I would have stood in front of him, performing high-pitched strangulated sounds and then galloping off like Dobbin. I reckon I would have been able to say, 'I have bought *The Complete Idiot's Guide to Tantric Sex*, would you like to do some of the exercises with me?' And I think I might have been able to receive his no, too. I remember at the time that he 'dumped me', Buddha in the Bedroom Next Door had exclaimed, 'This is such an amazing gift for you!' 'It's not a bloomin' gift, you knobhead!' I had thought. But post-Conscious Sexuality Festival I might have been capable of seeing it that way. I may even have been able to say, 'Fair enough, thanks for looking after yourself, I wish you well,' to the chap and meant it, rather than responding with drunken wailing and lots of languishing introspectively in bed.

The Love Lounge

In the evenings there were freer, less structured events like the kink party and the clothing-optional ecstatic dance party. Oh. Dear. Lord. Or you could hang out in the sauna or in the Love Lounge.

The Love Lounge was a big square tent with soft covered mattresses on the floor and richly coloured drapes around the walls. The light was dim and soft, low music played, and partially clothed or naked limbs writhed on the floor.

As you entered you might hear a murmur of pleasure; as

your eyes adjusted to the light you might catch sight of two men pleasuring a woman, a woman gasping as a man gently exposed her nipple and caressed it, or you might see two women sitting opposite each other laughing as they bounced their breasts together, or you might see two women leaning over a man, teasing his penis with their mouths.

If you had met someone you clicked with in a workshop you could invite them to the Love Lounge for some smooching. It wasn't by any means a complete free-for-all in there though. The room was run by probably the most warm and welcoming couple you could possibly meet. He, all cuddly physique and Cupid lips, topless in a waistcoat and comfy trousers, her with a flower in her wavy Titian hair and a long dress with full breasts spilling out. They showed you where to sit or lie and offered to administer cuddles, massages or caresses if desired. But, most importantly, they kept the space safe. There was also a safe word and action, 'Jellyfish,' shouted while waving your legs and hands in the air, so that if anything was happening that someone felt uncomfortable with, everything would be stopped and the situation dealt with.

When Bell Tent Man and I went to the Love Lounge, we lay down in a cosy corner, a sea of naked couples and groups all around us. Our mutual male friend was laid out nearby with a big erection and an attractive blonde woman. I thought it best not to wave.

We started kissing, but to be honest, the Love Lounge didn't feel like the place I wanted to be at that moment. I was aroused from a day at the festival.

'Let's not stay for long,' I whispered. 'I'd rather be in the tent where there's more room to get jiggy. It would be nice to be free to move around without kneeing another woman or getting a man's scrotum in my face. Call me fussy.'

He laughed. But then the woman I'd done the workshop with

on the first day walked in. Bell Tent Man knew her already, and said hello warmly to her.

'Do you know Lucy?' he said.

She looked at me and nodded.

'Oh, hello, we haven't met since we had a lovely time in a workshop,' I said.

We smiled and looked into each other's eyes.

'Would you like to join us?' I found myself asking her.

She nodded.

I suddenly remembered that Bell Tent Man should have a say in this too. 'Is that OK with you?'

He nodded, but then he more or less sat back and left us some space to greet each other. We smiled at each other and then leaned towards each other to kiss. I was so used to kissing stubbly men, she felt so soft and smooth in comparison.

We kissed for some time before drawing Bell Tent Man into our tryst. The three of us knelt on the soft floor. Three mouths, six hands, exploring, oh my goodness, it was dreamy. So soft, so slow. We drifted between each other with our hands and mouths. It was divine. I loved hearing her state her boundaries if something went too far – she was so in her own pleasure, and so kind and welcoming, and yet still so clear and strong if there was a touch she didn't want. A smile and a 'no', or a moved hand. It was very inspiring.

I gave her an orgasm with my fingers as she kissed Bell Tent Man. She moaned and gasped. The whole experience was very beautiful.

Women

When I sat down initially to do my Fuckit List, I'd had a light-bulb moment when it came to connecting physically with women.

'Duh! I fancy women. Why had I not realised this before?' They'd been all over my porn habits and fantasies for, well, ever, and crikey, I remember looking at the pictures of women in underwear in catalogues when I was little and, aged eight, I'd been caught playing with a girl's bum. Yes, whichever way I looked at it, I had been activated by women since childhood, but I'd somehow not linked all this with the fact that it might be nice to actually try exploring sexually with women. Weird.

That's not strictly true. Pre-sexual revolution I had partaken in a few sexual experiences with women, but the words which spring to mind when I think about them aren't 'erotic' and 'sensual'; they're more like 'drunk' and 'cringe'.

Once I had been at a party with my boyfriend at the time. We were in the kitchen chatting to a girlfriend and her boyfriend. Suddenly she leaned across the Formica kitchen surface towards me. 'Shall we snog?' she said. I nodded. We did.

Did I want to snog her? Coughs, looks down at shoes. No. Lucy, in your backstory, do you ever snog someone that you want to? Oh, bugger off. But the reason I snogged this girlfriend was different from the reason I snogged the litany of fellas I didn't want to snog. I snogged her because I thought it would turn my boyfriend on.

Later on he said, 'Why did you snog her? That was weird.'

'I thought it would turn you on.'

'It was just weird.'

'Oh.'

'Weird,' he said again, shaking his head.

Another incident occurred when I was reeeeally drunk, so drunk I was doing shots. A gay friend said, 'You're the straightest person I know.' The straightest person she knew! The STRAIGHTEST PERSON SHE KNEW! ME! So I snogged her, I guess in a bid to knock myself off that top spot. And because we were so preposterously pissed, we were horny, and ended up in bed together. At one point I remember saying, 'What do we do? Do we put things in each other?'

Now, I'm writing about all this, and wondering whether to use words like gay or straight or bi. I guess if someone made me choose a word it would be bi, but deep down I don't know what my sexuality is or if I ever really will know. For years and years, I've lived my life as a woman who has been told about sex and shown about sex from a man's perspective. What we generally see as 'normal' is a view of sex that has been created by heterosexual men for other heterosexual men: the daily image of the naked sixteen-year-old in the newspaper, the music videos, the big free porn sites. So I may have fallen into finding other women attractive because I was viewing it all like a heterosexual man. There weren't really many images of men around to turn me on, so I got turned on by all the images of women instead. I reckon I would get turned on by more sexy man stuff – I did, after all, have my first orgasm to a dancing Tarzan in cowboy boots. And I'm pretty sure I could look at Aidan Turner, or the Scottish actor Sam Heughan from *Outlander*, all day. I think what I am trying to say is that I have consumed so many images of 'beautiful' and/ or 'sexy' women that I am bound, on the one hand, to compare myself to them, as I did mercilessly and without question for well over thirty years, but I am also bound to get turned on by some of them too, because I am a sexual being.

So I don't know how much of me being attracted to women is because of society throwing lots of sexy images of women at me assuming I was a heterosexual man. BUT ALSO, sorry, this is about to get even more confusing, I don't know to what extent the fact that I dated and slept with men was down to the fact that since I was a little girl I'd been told that that is what women do. Without exception, pretty much all the stories I was told featured men and women together romantically. Had I been brainwashed into being straight by all the information around me, so much so that I completely ignored my feelings of arousal towards women?

Everything confused me. I didn't know what was real, or if I ever would. But I did so enjoy having sexual connections with women, and I had an inkling that my sexuality was far more fluid and interesting than I'd realised.

The Pussy Worship Workshop

Probably the most powerful experience for me at the festival was at the Pussy Worship Workshop. Now, this workshop had intrigued me. The word at the festival was that this was the one not one to miss. All you had to do was have a pussy and turn up to a big marquee with someone who was up for worshipping it for an hour and half. Bell Tent Man said he'd worship my pussy, so off we toddled.

I spoke to Marti Birch, one of the facilitators, afterwards. She said they had created the workshop because they 'wanted to give women permission to freely *express their sensual and sexual desires and be in charge of their own pleasure.*' And oh my goodness, I am so glad they did, because it felt seismic, life-changing and radical.

As with all the workshops, it started with very simple exercises to warm you up to the theme and connect you to yourself and other people. There was lots of simply staring into someone's eyes and practising the passing of power from one to the other, just being with the feeling of having dominance over another person, without actually 'doing' or saying anything. Then there was a situation where I was partnered with a young woman and I was holding dominance over her. I could ask/tell her to do anything. At one point, I asked/told her to crawl – really just because I had to find things for her to do, and there is only so much you can think of in a bare marquee. But as she crawled around on the floor before me I felt odd, uncomfortable, exploitative somehow. I felt protective of her, as though I didn't want her to humiliate herself for me. Afterwards we shared our experience and she said she had really enjoyed our session; she had trusted me and felt my kindness.

We moved on towards the long session with the partners we had come with, our pussy worshippers. To begin with, we were separated. The submissives were gathered together and taken outside by one teacher, and the dominants, the people with the pussies, were grouped together with another. We were led through some meditative exercises that focused on us being dominant, and were very still when our submissives were led back into the room. The one rule was: he couldn't do anything unless I told him to.

'Walk towards me.'

'Stop.'

'Lightly touch your fingers to my cheek.'

'Now my neck.'

'Put your hand in my hair and scratch my scalp.'

'Kiss me very softly once on the lips.'

'Move your hand gently over my breast.'

I loved taking things at my pace, oh so slowly at first, but then as I built up momentum, I found I wanted to lick his cheek, scratch him, slap him, take his clothes off. I surprised myself. I was animal. I gave him a blowjob and when I looked up at him he was looking down at me.

'Look out at the room,' I instructed him. I wanted him to look at all these other groups of people getting sexy while I pleasured him.

Then I took my own clothes off and lay down on the floor.

'Very slowly enter me.'

He penetrated me as I'd directed. And I suddenly let go and

sobbed. I spent the next ten minutes blubbing while he was inside me. I'd never get work doing improvisational porn.

I wept and wept. Who knows why? I think I had needed that experience so much, and it felt so overwhelming to be surrendered to in that way. I asked for a sexual experience exactly how I wanted it and someone gave it to me. I remember thinking at the time, 'Wow, this feels like love.'

Open relationship-ing

So there we were in our summer of love. I was in a relationship, and not just any relationship, an open one. Now, I had been very gung-ho about this. And in hindsight I should probably have thought it through a bit more, perhaps consulted people, checked a few 'what not to dos' with some experts. I mean, I'd proved myself fairly disastrous at having relationships with just the one person, I'm not sure why I thought it would be easy to bring in more. But I think you are probably getting to know me by now: I enthusiastically jump.

One of the problems might have had something to do with the fact that pre-sexy adventuring and getting to know Bell Tent Man, I didn't much like the word 'boundary'. It bored and annoyed me in equal measure. If I put a boundary around something, I was trapping it, limiting its freedom and its potential. BORRRING! I wanna be free, man. So boundary, schmoundary. It felt as though I had gone most of my life hearing the word only occasionally, and then suddenly it was everywhere.

Bell Tent Man and I had a run-in with the word fairly early on when he told me about a sex party he was planning to go to. He suggested we talk about boundaries first.

'I don't want to give you boundaries,' I said to him. 'I don't want to curtail you. If you really really want to do something, do it.'

Hmmm. I might not entirely have thought that one through.

He went to said party and things did indeed get sexy. And afterwards he told me about it over the phone. And at first it was OK.

'Ooo, I am so happy for you. That sounds lovely.'

And then there was a little throwaway: 'And I was just putting a condom on—'

'What?'

'Putting a—'

'Oh my God.'

'What?'

'Oh my God.'

'What?'

'Did you penetrate her?'

'Yes.'

Silence.

'Lucy, are you there?'

Well, fuckadoodle, it was all going on for me. I felt really, really red in the face, as though I was blushing like never before, and I couldn't really breathe very well either.

'I just . . . oh my God . . . it didn't even occur to me you'd do that.'

'But you should have said you didn't want me to do that . . .'

'It just never occurred to me you'd do that.'

It wasn't my finest hour. Perhaps there was something in this boundaries word after all.

'I would never want to hurt you. We'll make that a boundary in future.'

I stayed like that for ages, with flushed cheeks and an anxious knot in my chest, with the addition of lots of uncontrollable weeping.

I felt like a little girl who had been dancing away, showing everyone how happy she was, who suddenly tripped over and landed splat on concrete.

I just couldn't believe he would have had sex with someone else. I thought about when I was penetrated by him and how it was a such a massive, beautiful moment in our connection. He literally entered my body with his. I ached when I wasn't with him just to think of him penetrating me. How we took it slowly and looked into each other's eyes, how I felt the tip of his penis as it slid inside me and then the width of the shaft as it travelled up me. It really hadn't occurred to me that he would do that with someone else. Was I out of my depth? This hurt.

But then I started to understand a bit more of the other side when I had a lovely spontaneous connection with a very sexy man a few weeks later. I didn't have penetrative sex, but I did enjoy an orgasm, and lots of kissing and caressing. Wow. And my partner was OK with this! No! He was actually happy for me. Wahoo! Open relationship-ing, where have you been all my life?

I was high as a kite for a day or two. New relationship with man I was falling in love with? Tick. Shenanigans with another sexy fella? ANOTHER TICK! I was like some sort of legendary defier of female conditioning! Roar. But then I started to notice something. Hmmm. This wasn't in the plan. I kept thinking about the other guy – I wasn't thinking about Bell Tent Man so much. And that made me . . . angry. But, the thing is, I don't generally get angry. In fact, I've probably been angry about five times in my whole life. So when I do get angry I find it exciting. Thrilling, even. But it's not focused, contained, manageable anger. Do you know of the Hindu goddess Kali with the necklace of skulls? Yeah, my anger was a bit more like that. 'What are we doing?' I wanted to bellow. 'We should be protecting our relationship!' It felt as though we were feeding it to the lions.

This open relationshipping wasn't one for the quiet life, I noted.

The sex party

Shortly after the festival Bell Tent Man and I went to a sex party. It wasn't in nature, sadly, I had yet to come across one of those, but was in a beautiful stately home surrounded by nature where people could camp. Fancy dress was mandatory and the theme, as far as I could tell, was sophisticated ghostly chic. This was a problem for me: if it doesn't involve borrowing my friend's Kermit costume, then I don't do fancy dress. And it just felt *wrong* to take Kermit to a sex party. After some frenzied last-minute shopping in a small village not known for its shopping potential, I ended up going as Miss Havisham in her pants. This was purely because I found a pair of silk French knickers, a veil and some long satin gloves in the corner of an antique shop. I teamed them with a lot of long beads and necklaces and a pair of high Victorian-ish black boots.

It is fair to say that there was something slightly hysterical about Lucy arriving at a sex party. When I am excited and nervous I don't speak a lot, but when I do words come out very, very fast and oddly I sound much posher than usual. I was all about the self-love so I felt oddly affectionate towards my own lack of cool; it even made me chuckle. But all this meant that I arrived at said sex party dressed like a topless Miss Havisham, strangely bemused by myself and hysterical when approached.

There was mingling and cabaret in the sumptuous downstairs and then, as the night progressed, upstairs was made available for frolicking. These upstairs rooms had a Moulin Rouge boudoir vibe, with far more beds and red velvet drapes than you tend to find in most bedrooms, and were soundtracked by an erotic Café del Mar-style mix.

We wandered upstairs when it was still fairly quiet. We found a spot big enough for the two of us on the huge bed.

I think to get a bed so huge they had joined lots of doubles together, topped them with foam and then sheeted them. I explain this because I want you to know that when I say 'huge bed' I don't just mean a generous king, I mean a bed that filled an entire room in a stately home. We chatted briefly to a smiling man, naked except for his dog collar. A buxom woman was giving him the odd slap on his pink bottom. We saw a couple we knew. They were kissing. We rolled towards them and said hello. We chatted for a while and then found ourselves in a little huddle, sharing little kisses and friendly touches. It felt innocent and tender. We got a little bit undressed – well, they did, I was fairly undressed to begin with. No one motored to orgasm, rather we just gently bobbed around for quite some time in those lovely sensations of arousal.

There was one point where I felt a tad out of the action as the other three were all occupied. I looked about me. A beautiful young couple were having sex next to me; she was on top, very slowly riding him. She smiled at me, slowly leaning towards me. I smiled back. We seemed to drift into each other somehow, and then we kissed. It was such a simple, natural, lovely moment. I stayed kissing her for some time.

'Would you like me to touch your breasts?' I asked, thinking that it would probably feel good while she was being penetrated.

'Yes.'

I caressed and kissed her. She smiled dreamily at me and moaned.

'I'd better get back to my group,' I whispered after a little while. 'I think I may have been a bit rude buggering off there. Have a lovely evening.'

It was strange. I didn't feel out of my depth in this situation at all. I felt confident; in my element, in fact. The rest of my buddy group welcomed me back afterwards for more huddling.

Another couple I recognised had established themselves near

us. He seemed kind and mischievous and I thought she was beautiful, with a lovely big smile that made me smile too. I felt very drawn to her warmth. As far as I could tell, the two of them often operated in a power-play routine where she was totally submissive to him.

I leaned over to them, smiling and saying hello. Then, jumping into their role play, I asked him if I could kiss her. He said yes, but told her she wasn't allowed to come until he told her to.

We kissed and stroked and smiled for some time and then Bell Tent Man and I drifted away from this scenario. The two of us snuggled, kissed and nattered. We'd been in there for a few hours by this point and I had started to feel woozy. I'd come over all faint, like a Jane Austen character, possibly from being so aroused for so long.

'I need some air.'

The hardest part was finding all the bits of my costume I'd discarded along the way. My hair and convent education were at this point quite dishevelled.

I lay like a lolloping whale on the grass outside for some time. Bell Tent Man fetched me water, and concerned partygoers approached from time to time to check I was OK. It was pretty late by the time I had cooled down and revived. We wondered whether to call it a night, but decided instead to have one last look in on the party before heading to bed.

We found a spot in a different room this time. A man tenderly penetrated a woman on all fours nearby. The friends we had smooched with were one couple over. We waved, but started to have a bit of a kiss and a cuddle on our own, thinking we might just have sex there, the two of us, and head homewards.

Soon, before we'd really got going, a very beautiful woman reached out to me and the two of us started kissing. Her partner was on top of her, my partner on top of me. The rest is a bit of a blur of bodies to be honest.

I remember a really lovely chap with a massive penis and smile asking, 'Can I watch?'

'Yes,' I replied.

'It's so hot.' He admired the scene.

'I know!' I whooped.

A few moments passed.

'Can I play with your nipples?'

'Oh, I would love that, thank you!'

What a nice fella.

I remember squealing, 'OH MY GOD!!! SHE'S PUT HER FINGER UP MY BUM!!' at one point. (It turns out that screeching, 'OH MY GOD!!! SHE'S PUT HER FINGER UP MY BUM!!' adequately halts that particular insertion.) And I remember Bell Tent Man's upside-down face appearing at another and asking, 'Can you breathe at that angle?' I was very touched by that.

The evening had a strange and interesting effect on me. I became, erm, there's no other word for it, insatiable. We went back to our tent that night and had sex. I awoke early the next morning wanting more sex. Bell Tent Man was worried about chafing, but kindly obliged me with an orgasm as I replayed scenes from the night before in my mind, and then a female friend stopped by to say hello, and we (well, mainly me) invited her to join us in more lovemaking. It was as though the more I had, the more I wanted. I had never experienced anything like it.

It was like I was high, though I hadn't even had an alcoholic drink the night before, let alone any other substances. But although feeling high can be exciting and energetic, I also felt a little unhinged and unwieldy. It took a few days for me to calm down and find myself back at my normal equilibrium, and I was relieved to land there again.

Consent, consent and a bit more consent

One thing that struck me again and again was how all these sexual shenanigans rested on and revolved around the giving and receiving of consent. But consent was recognised as not just being as simple as a yes or a no. For a start it was an ongoing conversation, liable to change at any point. It was also acknowledged that participants could struggle with aspects of this negotiation, either with expectations or with speaking up. It was not simply assumed that everyone was super powerful and assertive at all times.

I've pinched part of what I think is an incredible 'consent in practice guidelines' document for the Summer House Weekend (a sex-positive summer festival). This is just a fraction of a much longer text which I think is bloomin' amazing (the authors are the Summer House, Kinky Salon London and Pink Therapy).

Making and receiving approaches
- If you'd like any kind of touch or encounter with somebody, ask the other person **once** before doing anything or inviting them to participate. Examples: 'Mind if we sit here?' 'May I give you a hug?' 'Would you like to dance?' 'Care to come to the playroom with me?' etc.
- If you're suggesting a kink scene of any kind then make sure you're clear about exactly what it would involve, and how experienced you are, so that the other person can make **informed consent**.
- Unless you get a fully enthusiastic response such as **'yes please'** then say 'no worries' and drop the subject (or move away if the person seems at all uncomfortable). Many people, perhaps the majority, feel uncomfortable saying 'no'.
- **Watch out for the many subtle ways of saying no,** such as 'Not now', 'You're not my type', 'I like you but', 'I'm not

sure', 'You've/I've been drinking', 'Maybe later'. If someone looks uncertain, makes an excuse, or says anything that is not an enthusiastic 'yes', take their uncertainty as a no.

- **Remember that some people are given different degrees of 'permission' by society to ask for what they want or don't want.** So pay attention to the other person when talking about what you do or don't want. Who is doing most of the talking? Is there a sense of enthusiasm? Are they going along with the conversation because they are finding it too awkward?
- The following differences between you might complicate the ease with which someone can feel comfortable saying no: one of you being older or more experienced; one of you being a facilitator or organiser at an event; differences in gender, race, ethnicity, disability status, class, education, language; differences that mean that one of you is generally seen as less culturally 'attractive' and/or differences in levels of self-confidence or mental-health struggles.
- **When someone does say no, it definitely means no** – and this can happen at any time of an encounter. The **only** exception is where you have both specifically agreed a safe word taking the place of 'no' that everyone can use to bring all play to an end.[1]

What I love, love, LOVE about this is the acknowledgement that power dynamics can influence our ability to give clear consent. It doesn't assume that we are all on a level playing field.

My mind was blown yet further on this subject when I went to a talk about something called the Wheel of Consent. This was devised by an American chiropractor and intimacy coach called Betty Martin. I'm going to try and explain a bit about it here, but PLEASE look it up yourself and have a read, Betty gives away a lot of information about this online. The basic gist of the Wheel of Consent is that in every encounter involving touch, someone is doing and someone is having something done *to* them, but the doer can be doing it either for their own benefit or for their partner's.

Everything here is consensual, but there is more than consent in place.

Have a look at the diagram below (and thank you, Betty, for letting me copy it here).[2]

Betty says it's not just about permission – it goes deeper than that. The agreement includes not just what is going to happen, but who it's for. The four states of being in all this are to allow, to serve, to accept and to take. The basic idea is that if you serve or allow, it is for the other person. If you take or accept, it is for you.

Let me try to break this down a bit, as I understand it.

To serve: You are doing what the other person wants. It is about them. It might start with a 'Would you like a massage?' or the other person might make the request, 'Could you go down on me?', for example. In order to serve them fully you need to check that they are enjoying themselves (unless they are making so many appreciative noises that you are absolutely in no doubt). You do this by communicating questions such as 'Is this what you had in mind?', 'Would you like me to touch you here?', 'Is there anything you'd like different?' etc.

To accept: This is where the other person is doing what you want. It's about you. You have a large responsibility to create the pleasurable experience that you desire and that the person serving you seeks to give you. So again communication is key. 'Ooo, lovely. Thank you.' Or, 'No, could you touch me like this, please.' 'A little gentler/harder.' 'Can you pause for a moment?' 'Hmmm. That is fucking amazing.' And so on.

To take: This is where you are doing what you want. It's for you, for your enjoyment. You have probably experienced this when you feel someone's body because you like the way it feels to you, or maybe you were on top and wildly rocking towards your own orgasm.

To allow: This is where your partner is doing what they want and you are fine with it. It's about them (though it can feel great to you too!). In allowing, you 'give' your body. Maybe they want to feel you up or play with your hair. The steamy Mills & Boon fantasy of being ravished sees the woman allowing and enjoying it.

These four areas are always in play. But a lot of time we unconsciously flick about the wheel, and it was this unconscious flicking that was where historically my sex got a bit complicated. In most of my sexual encounters I had been in the serving and allowing roles. But a lot of the time my sexual experiences became muddied and complicated generally because someone had started giving me pleasure, meaning I was in the accepting role, but this would shift when I stopped enjoying it. I wouldn't say anything, but I would feel like he was taking, although he still thought he was serving.

I loved learning about all this, and became committed to trying to go against my natural tendency to be passive, and to speak up and make clear agreements when it came to sex.

BDSM

How are you doing? Still here? All OK? Sorry, it's all me, me, me, isn't it, this book?

I was cracking on with my list. Hitherto I'd thought of BDSM as 'punishment sex'. I think it was the props that did it, the whips and chains and the fact that it took place in a dungeon. I've never been one to willingly opt for pain. I'm more of a 'take me to the bliss' kind of person. All the leather and straps felt like the antithesis to the scented-candle softness and 'relaxing sensual massage' playlists I had been rather enjoying.

Still, I was an intrepid explorer and I wanted to find out more because I realised that I knew very little about it.

I didn't even know what the letters stood for. So I did a bit of the old online research and found out that BDSM is an amalgamation of abbreviations. B&D (bondage and discipline), D&S (domination and submission), and S&M (sadism and masochism).

Bondage and discipline: this sounded quite straightforward, bondage being restraints, handcuffs and stuff, and discipline, well that's rules, punishment and the like. Domination and submission, I guessed was all master and servant, teacher/pupil, that sort of malarkey. And then there was S&M. Now, the words sadism and masochism, I found out via Wikipedia, come from two dudes, the Marquis de Sade and Leopold von Sacher-Masoch. So I idly did an internet search to find out more about the Marquis de Sade, and shitting hell!!! I mean, possibly my first stop shouldn't have been a *Vice* article, because I learned that soon after he was married, he took a prostitute called Jeanne Testard home. He asked her if she believed in God and then 'shoved pieces of communion host inside her vagina', and screwed her, shouting, 'If thou art God, avenge yourself!' After that, 'he went on to masturbate with two crucifixes and attempt to give her an enema so she would shit in a holy chalice, all the while referring to Jesus as a "motherfucker" and the Virgin Mary as a "buggress".'[1]

Apparently, he 'theorised that because women can fake pleasure but not pain, the latter must be the higher form of sexual activity.' Oookay.

It was with a little trepidation I looked up the other fella, Leopold von Sacher-Masoch. I learned that he was a writer who wrote a novella called *Venus in Furs*, published in 1870, which was about a chap who had a relationship with a woman where he became her servant. 'Trample on me!' he demands.

Riiiight. I sat down and thought about these words, bondage and discipline, submission and domination, and what, if anything, I might want to experience in the realms of BDSM. Another list. Here we go.

1. I wanted someone to play with my pleasure

I realised that I was VERY up for submitting to someone IF I trusted them and if they were going to give me pleasure. I did not, however, fancy submitting to someone who wanted to bang on about God while giving me an enema. Someone was very welcome to take me beyond the pleasure I'd already known so that I would feel quivery, sweaty, panting and spent afterwards. Yep, I was happy to surrender to someone else's dominance and be submissive for this, because I wanted this experience of intense pleasure. But I wondered whether I was getting the hang of this BDSM thing, because as you've doubtless gathered, it was pleasure I was seeking here, NOT pain.

2. I thought I may as well have a go at being a dominatrix
I wasn't exactly keen. It didn't turn me on. It didn't feel very me. I had a feeling I would be fairly ridiculous at it. I had visions of trying it and feeling as though I was stuck in a surreal comedy, unable to get out. Standing there, PVC and dread creating the perfect terrain for thrush, whip sliding in my sweaty palms, a man at my feet, bottom in the air. Still, this was my sexual adventure, and I felt I should have a go.

3. Spanking
It dawned on me that I'd never been spanked. Although I do remember one time when I was sitting on someone's face and he suddenly gave me a slap on a bum cheek. Ooo, I'm feeling a bit tingly thinking about it now.

Spanking

I leaned over the kitchen table.

'Er. Can you just give my bottom a little spank?' I asked.

Bell Tent Man's answer was a cupped hand on my buttock. And then another.

On and on, he continued.

'Thank you,' I said, when I didn't want to be spanked any more. 'That's enough, now.'

And, I rather liked it. I found it was energising. I had been feeling sluggish, fuggish, generally of the morning 'urgh', but the spanking cleansed all of this and left me feeling alive and revitalised. It took me from the natter of my thoughts, straight and quickly to my physical experience. It's hard to worry about the washing-up when your bum is on fire. 'Be here, now, you with the tingly arse', the spanking seemed to say.

I felt quite high after my impromptu spanking session.

Apparently, this is because the body produces endorphins in response to pain and I knew enough about endorphins to know that I bloomin' loved them. They are pretty much the body's natural morphine. Endorphins are released when you exercise, dance, make love, breastfeed a baby, even eat chocolate. I am a major fan. More please, more. But now I was learning that these little wonders also flood the body in response to pain, which means that there actually is pleasure in pain. And I found this fact slightly alarming. It's a bit dangerous to digest. If more pain = more endorphins, that meant that more pain = more pleasure. Well, then, how far would I be willing to go with this?

Hang about though, when I hurt myself in my everyday life, I don't usually enjoy it. We don't tend to stand there repeatedly stubbing our toes in order to feel the endorphins, do we? No, but people do bend over and have their bottom spanked or flogged, and this is because not only do they get the endorphin buzz, they get a rush of blood to their pelvic or sex region. Oh, it's making sense now, isn't it? Bottom spanking for pleasure is sounding like the most sensible thing in the world now, isn't it?

And yet, there was a little worry about all this niggling at me. It had to do with the potential for exploitation. The line between love and passionate loathing can be thin and wiggly, and I don't really fancy having someone take out their bad day at work/the fact I locked them out last night/their relationship with their mother on my bottom. We often play out our weird stuff in sex and relationships, and people can be cruel. There seemed to be great potential for someone to whack me about and then say, 'I hurt you for your pleasure, I am exonerated of wrongdoing.'

Was I thinking this because I distrust people? Or was it more that I distrusted myself? If I thought back to how long it had taken me to find my voice and my 'no'. I could imagine that if I had stumbled across BDSM earlier, with my desperation to please and be desired, I might have got myself in situations that I may have regretted later. I had already got myself into sexual situations I hadn't really wanted to be in because I didn't like/wasn't able to say no or stop, so who is to say I wouldn't have got myself into sexually violent or painful situations for the same reasons? Trust. It came back to trust. I would reeeeeally need to trust someone, and myself, to start playing around with the pain thang.

That first spot of spanking wasn't a sexual experience though. More a little pick-me-up. Cheaper and quicker to the vein than a coffee. Curious about sexing it up, I did a quick bit of internet research and learned not to spank above the buttocks, where the kidneys are located, as it could cause internal damage. And also, very excitingly, I learned that there is a sweet spot for spanking. Oh, I do love a sweet spot. It is the area where the skin is thinner at the top of the thighs and lower buttocks, the inner area near the bum crevice. Makes sense really as it's the bit of your bum that is near the genitals. I also came across the rather lovely term 'spankophile'.

All the articles stress taking your time and paying close attention to when it becomes too much, and always speaking up if it isn't working for you. If you enter into a role-play situation you must always have a safe word that has been agreed beforehand and can be said at any time to stop proceedings. This can be anything, PINEAPPLE or JUSTIN BIEBER, but is very often RED or SAFE WORD. Often people use a traffic-light system, where RED would stop activity straight away, and YELLOW means 'slow down' or 'ease up'.

I started to ask Bell Tent Man for a little bit of a spank here and there. It became a fun way to connect, a shared moment between doing the dishes and *I'm a Celebrity*. As I started to understand and enjoy how vital I felt after a little bottom smack it popped up in lovemaking more too, and seemed to maximise pleasure in both foreplay and intercourse. I felt my nerve endings come alive. It felt as though I had thousands of throbbing nerve endings! And that was because I do actually HAVE thousands of throbbing nerve endings!! He-e-e-e-llo.

We bought a flogger online and started using that here and there too. The strips of leather awakened my whole body. Well, faux leather. It was a bit of a shit one, to be honest, but enough to get the idea. You see, you could spend a fortune on the kit. There are people crafting absolutely beautiful BDSM products: nipple clamps that look like jewellery, bespoke floggers made from deerskin, vintage paddles (not to be confused with the long ones used for rowing). In fact, go on Etsy and you'll see pages and pages of paddles. So many paddles for sale I started to think that I must be the only person who doesn't own one. Honestly, there are so many pages of paddles it gave me some major FOMO, and I added 'buy a personalised paddle' to the list of things I will do when I have money.

Bell Tent Man and I were still at the shallow, or comedy, end of the spanking spectrum, but I was aware that there was much further that we could go with this sort of 'impact play' if we wanted to. Aficionados of BDSM and spanking speak about how spanking can be controlled and built upon so that the submissive can enter a subspace where they are pretty much zonked out by the pleasure/pain combo. That felt like it was going too far for me. I was interested in experiencing some of it, but I didn't want to go the whole gaga. I asked myself why that was. And I think I was scared. On the one hand, I like altered states of consciousness. I used to get in this state with booze, fags and recreational drugs, but now I prefer the natural and free methods like meditation, dancing and orgasm. But do I want to cultivate a relationship with spanking, adrenalin and endorphins? Not really. I will dabble a little, but experiencing this subspace doesn't entirely feel like my thing.

Still, I was curious to experience more impact play. Funny

how the world of BDSM was already pulling me further in than I'd intended to go with my original little list. But impact play was an area that Bell Tent Man wasn't particularly into, and I felt I probably needed to go to an expert to get the kind of introduction to BDSM and impact play that I was looking for.

Bell Tent Man and I discussed this. He wasn't comfortable with the thought of me going off to be slapped on the bum with various bits of equipment by some random dude. His fear was that the chap would be a bit psycho-ish and cruel, I wouldn't be able to find my 'no' and would end up having an experience that wasn't great for me. But he thought about it and in the end suggested I approach someone we both knew, who had taught some workshops at the Conscious Sexuality Festival, and ask him if he could give me an intro session. He was a really friendly, kind and approachable chap with the most handsome, lovely face, who really knew his stuff. My partner trusted him completely. I typed him a Facebook message explaining what I wanted, and he came back with a big yes, having felt honoured and thrilled to be asked.

Meeting a fella to have my bottom spanked

I went to his house for the session. We sat at first, discussing the area he lived in and my journey over biscuits and coffee, while a punishment pole with a pink fluffy collar and a spanking bench stood winking at me from his conservatory. Nearby, an old-fashioned coat stand was draped with whips and floggers. Rather than looking terrifying, it looked gorgeous. I wanted one for my living room. A flogger in the softest raspberry leather, a candyfloss-pink feather tickler, a heart-shaped paddle. This was less terrifying dungeon, more drama play with the kids.

He had a big checklist that we went through together, so that I was able to create a session that worked for me. There were some things on the list that I hadn't heard of, and some I definitely didn't want to explore.

DS checklist – ecstasy and intimacy

Locations	Intensity/Duration	Score
Front, Back Arms, Legs Feet, Hands Face, Head Breast, Nipples Bum, Genitals 'Visible' areas	Hard, Medium, Soft Plenty, Some, A Little	0 – Don't know, but try (go gently . . .) 1 – Favourite/I love it! 2 – Please include this 3 – Neutral 4 – Minimal, if at all/ punishment 5 – Definitely not!

Activity	Location(s) YES or NO or MAYBE (soft limit)	Intensity/Duration	Score
Sensations:			
Stroke			
Scratch			
Pinch			
Squeeze/Pressure			
Slap			
Spank			
Bite			
Hair-pull			

Punch			
Leave marks?			
Toys:			
Flogger (thuddy)			
Flogger (stingy)			
Paddle (soft)			
Paddle (hard)			
Soft toy (mitt)			
Cane			
Vampire gloves			
Clothes pegs			
Nipple clamps			
Pinwheel			
Temperature Play:			
Wax			
Ice			
Flash cotton			
Fireplay			
Power Play:			
Collar			
Lead			
Blindfold			
Handcuffs			
Spanking bench			

Punishment post			
Verbal Commands:			
Walk, be led			
Sit, kneel, lie			
Remove clothing			
Fetch things			
Speak, e.g. 'yes, sir'			
Humiliation			
Role play			
Safety:			
Any injuries, etc.?	Where? Discuss implications		
Safe words, e.g.:	Orange = 'At limit but keep going' Red = 'Stop and check in, may or may not start again'		
Open and close	Start with three breaths together and eye contact. End with three breaths together and eye contact.		
Power/equality	Feel into and verbally hand over power at the start of the ritual, and return it at the end of the ritual.		
Aftercare	Anything you know you'll need? Allow enough time.		
Debrief	Debrief afterwards, using this chart for guidance.		

For the first part of the session he talked me through each 'toy' and he allowed me to experience it making contact with my body. I either stood with my hands above my head and resting on a wall, or lay down on a bed. There was a lot of communication: 'This is the thuddy flogger, how is that?' 'Mmm, nice.' 'How about here?' 'Mmmm, yes, helloo.' 'What about a little harder?' I was quite vocal with my enjoyment, 'Ah, ah, ooo, ahhh,' and I used 'Orange' when I needed to, appreciating having a word that meant 'This is pretty much all I can take with this, but don't stop!' He'd intersperse a flogger with a quick all-over stroking with a soft furry mitt. I didn't like the wax, but I bloomin' loved the vampire gloves, black leather gloves with little spikes on, which made your whole body tingle and vibrate. At the end of the session I felt spoiled and pampered beyond belief. This BDSM malarkey was continually surprising me.

After lunch, I was chained to the punishment post and bent over the spanking bench. I was more uneasy then; there was something of humiliation in the pose which made me feel more vulnerable and self-conscious. I had less control, I guess. I liked the sensations of the contact that the toys made with my body, but was less comfortable in these positions. I giggled, a bit embarrassed.

I had felt a bit helpless, and I hadn't particularly liked it. For years, I realised, I had felt largely helpless and submissive in terms of sex and relationships; perhaps this was why I didn't particularly want to play at submitting to a guy now.

Me as a dominant

When I was at the Conscious Sexuality Festival, I'd gone to what was referred to as a Play Party (not to be confused with something you'd take a toddler to) and had an experience of being in the dominatrix role.

A chap I knew had a fondness for being spanked, and was happy to lend his bottom to me. There was a table of props at the side of the room. Nipple clamps, paddles, straps, crops, floggers, it was quite the array of paraphernalia. I picked up a cat o' nine tails.

The young man was already on his hands and knees before

me. He was wearing a kilt. Handy. He lifted the skirt to reveal his buttocks. Golly. He was keen.

'This is the first time I've ever done this!' I shouted, shrilly. I don't think shrill was the ideal vocal characteristic for the occasion. I flicked my wrist back.

'Oh shit!! Sorry! Did I hit you?!' I screeched. I thought I'd clipped the beautiful woman wearing just a rope behind me. 'Are you OK?'

She was fine. Phew.

'Sorry,' I said to the fella on the floor. 'Right, bear with me.' I sighed, preparing myself for another go.

Leather meets flesh. Thwack.

'OH MY GOD!!! ARE YOU OK???' I shrieked, crouching down to talk to the chap.

However I was soon to hear about a workshop, which, when I read the blurb, made my whole body and mind do a rousing YESSSSS. 'In Love and Service' was run by a woman called Ruby May and was being held in London over a weekend.

It was described as being a 'workshop exploring the erotic alchemy of female dominance and male service and its potential for pleasure, expansion and personal and collective healing.'

This had MY NAME ON IT!! Punching the air, I was.

The website went on to say:

As a woman in the leadership position, we learn to connect deeply with ourselves, our desires and inner wisdom. We practise cultivating confidence, and learn to find ease and joy in our communication. Our assertiveness might lead us to ask for exactly the touch we crave, or lead us into focusing on and enjoying our submissive in exactly the ways we choose, perhaps discovering the 'penetrator' or 'ravisher' in us.[2]

The workshop sold out in a matter of hours. I made sure I got a place. I couldn't wait. I was soooooo EXCITED! I then got the briefing email ten days before with all the details about travel and timings and a list of what to bring. This list ranged from 'notebook and pen' and 'bottle of water' to 'something sexy to wear' (crikey and bugger, I always found that tricky) to 'strap-on and lube'. Sorry, what was that last one? I'd come a long way on my sexual journey, but I wasn't sure I was at the 'strap-on and lube' stage yet.

Riiiiiiight. Ooooookay. And shiiiiiiiiiit.

Reading on, I learned that on the Sunday there would be a 'female-to-male penetration ritual', and I started to panic. As ever, my panicking habit led me to do absolutely nothing for over a week, save panic. Then the day before the workshop started I decided, 'I should get a strap-on, the course sounds amazing, I wouldn't want to miss out on this FEMALE-TO-MALE PENETRATION RITUAL WITH A STRAP-ON.' Brief pause for more panicking. I found the nearest Ann Summers and went there.

'Can I help you?' the assistant asked.

'I'd like a strap-on, please.' I said, sounding far more caj than someone who had been hyperventilating about strap-ons for the last eight days.

'Here are the belts,' she said.

I only noticed the cheapest (life is easier that way), a belt with canvas camping straps attached to a faux-leather pad with a silver hoop.

'And these are the dildos.'

Now, there might have been some smaller ones, some that were a bit more refined, say, or more hospitable, but it was Mr Dick, the humungous, veiny, realistic latex penis complete with scrotum that caught my eye.

I pulled Mr Dick out of the box when I got home. He felt

lovely, like a stress-reliever toy. There was a sucker on his base so you could stick him to your desk or the side of the bath, fridge, anywhere. I was smitten.

Bell Tent Man looked at Mr Dick and winced.

'Oof, that's big. I don't think many guys will want that up their . . .'

Ah, yes, he had a point.

'I think that's probably for a woman's vagina,' he added.

'Oh, bollocks, I've only gone and bought the wrong sodding dildo.'

The weekend was being held in a very large room in south London. It was a scary door to open. I was on my own, Bell Tent Man wasn't able to join me. I was definitely more confident by this point, but is anyone really confident all the time? I guess there will always times when I will feel more self-conscious than others, and entering a workshop with Mr Dick in my knapsack was one of those times.

The thing about these environments is that in my head beforehand everyone is uber-confident, gorgeous and looks witheringly at me and my terrible lack of cool. But in reality we are all there, fabulous in our flawed-ness. We're all a little nervous and anticipatory, and that shows up in a variety of ways. For some it is looking aloof, for some it is non-stop smiles and chatter, and for others it is sitting quietly with their eyes closed. We were all there to explore a little bit of ourselves that we were curious about. As it was, I instantly bumped into a funny female buddy who I hadn't seen for aeons. I started to feel at home very quickly.

Like the other workshops I had been to, there was a good selection of herbal teas, quite a lot of dark chocolate being offered around and a fair few blankets were being worn as shawls.

Now I am going to tell you a bit about this workshop, but I must point out that that there is a confidentiality agreement in workshops like this, so while I can tell you some bits and tell you how I felt and what I learned, there are some parts that aren't only my stories to tell.

Female erotic leadership workshop

Some of the main exercises we did in the workshop were:

1) The women sat on chairs in a large circle, and the men stood inside the circle, each facing a woman sitting down. The men had to do what the women wished, but the women could only use sign language to show them what this was. Each woman had three minutes with each man, after which a bell sounded. Then the women stayed where they were and the men moved on to the next woman.

2) Men were asked to spread out in the room and sit on the floor with their eyes closed. The women then sat next to the man they would like to work with. The couple created a 'nest', a comfortable space with cushions and blankets. Then they had forty-five minutes where the man asked, 'What do you desire?' to the woman, who then stated what she desired in that moment. These couldn't be things that were impossible to provide, i.e. 'to be on the beach', but rather things like 'just to sit here for a moment and not have to do anything', or, 'I would love for you massage my head', or, 'could you spank/kiss/sing to me', etc.

3) The men and women were separated. The women's group put on their strap-ons, while the men sat in a circle to discuss penetration. The women walked around the space checking out each other's 'penises' and seeing how wearing a cock like this changed how they felt and moved. Then the men were led into the space.

4) The very last exercise was the penetration ritual. This was an opportunity to explore female-to-male penetration either in pairs or groups. Penetration could be energetic – transmitting energy from one to the other – or with words, or with more physical contact. The space was equipped with condoms, gloves, lube, etc., and was sex-friendly, if that was what you wanted to do, but by no means was it mandatory or expected.

I think the main thing I got from this weekend was being given the opportunity over three days to practise having control and power. Being assertive, or at least not being passive, was, for me at least, like learning any other new skill: it took practise. Although there were a few other things that I discovered that weekend:

1. When I am tuned in to what I want and am feeling powerful, I take my time

When I had the power in these exercises, often I was quite still. I would connect to him in this stillness. It struck me that the world is man-made and is too bloomin' fast for me. We're so caffeinated and rushed all the time. Often there is so much talk and information coming at me that I literally cannot think. I have to step back and quieten everything down so that I can FEEL. And if I think about sex, so many of my sexual experiences over the years felt as though I was constantly being pushed by a guy to go a bit further. I'd felt it sooooo many times over sooooo many years. I'd be having a good time getting to know a guy and then he'd come on strong and suddenly it was all about sex; I often felt as though I was being rushed (the speed thing again) towards something I wasn't ready for or didn't want at all. Either I'd carry on, not saying anything, or I would extricate myself from the tryst, but with the latter came this heavy, shitty sense that I had really disappointed the guy.

What I loved about doing these exercises where I had the power was that I got used to slowing things down. If I started to lose myself at any point, or feel as though things were moving too fast, I would simply pause, breathe, take a sip of tea, and even say, 'I just need a few moments,' or 'I'm just going to press pause for a second, and see how I am feeling.' I think they are better responses than 'SLOW DOWN YOU RANDY GOAT AND GET THAT FINGER OUT OF THERE NOW!' or my historical fallback position of carrying on while not feeling great, which is shite for all involved.

2. I wasn't used to asking myself what I wanted
This actually brings me to another thing that made me teary.

During the course of the exercise I got a little annoyed with the 'What do you desire?' question. Sometimes I just didn't want anything, I was content as I was, and I felt the question was hurrying me (there we go again), trying to move me on to something else, maybe sex. I had to really think, 'What do I want?' and the question felt so bloomin' unfamiliar that it did my head in. I didn't generally know what I wanted because I was so unused to asking myself, because I WAS TOO FUCKING BUSY WORRYING ABOUT WHETHER I WAS WANTED OR WHAT THE OTHER PERSON MIGHT WANT. When I was asked what I desired, I couldn't grasp the scope of all that I *could* want and achieve. And that made me angry, and then very sad.

3. That being a woman in the dominant role doesn't have to look like Mistress Whiplash and inflict a lot of pain
I think the only vision I had had of women in an erotic leadership role was of this caricature. But this workshop helped

me find a different way. I didn't have to shout abuse at anyone, I could just be me and find my own take on it and what felt right for me.

Oh crikey, I've got a penis

So I put on Mr Dick. How did I feel? Most definitely different. I moved differently. I took my time (here we go) and played with the guys. My strap-on was the biggest. Guys looked unnerved. One saw it and then literally did a little cartoon skip to back away from me. I found myself walking closer to men than I would have done before. Oh, I'm almost resisting saying it, as seems so trite, but I felt POWERFUL. I had this thing and it was king. Cock power. I led from it.

However, when I did interact physically with men, something else happened. There was this big dangly weight in front of me and I became aware that this thing could hurt. It felt in some ways as though I had a weapon. I know this is sounding weird – please bear with me, as I think it's about to get weirder. I also felt that when I was close to someone I was able to access a really beautiful tenderness too. It was the realisation that I could be very strong but very tender. Even when a man's head was pressed to my strap-on penis (very hot) and I pulled his hair, I was tender. It was as though I knew that this thing could hurt, and if it did, I wanted it to be the most conscious, kindest, sweetest kind of pain. It was mind-exploding.

I did find myself thinking about men's response to being penetrated by Mr Dick, though. Mr Dick is a realistic member, bigger than average, yes, but not out of the realms of possibility. I would say Mr Dick is just ever so slightly bigger than the main penis I hang out with.

The guys seemed, understandably I'd say, pretty terrified of Mr Dick entering them anally. And I found myself getting a bit annoyed and angsty about this this fact. Women are expected to take these same big penises up their anuses – no dainty dildos are offered instead. In the past, I've had men try to enter my anus with their well-endowed penises without lube as though it was no big deal, and I'm reminded of that expression 'smash her back doors in' – sorry, but what the actual fuck.

I found an interesting blog post by Ruby May called 'On Penetration':[3]

I wouldn't go as far as to say that I'd never have anal sex with a man who hasn't been penetrated himself . . .

But I find it so amazing how obvious the difference is between men who have been penetrated themselves and men who haven't.

There is something about a man who has embodied the surrendering and opening and trust that's required in anal penetration, who has been able to discern conditioning from truth around being a 'real' man and is so comfortable in his skin, and in his manhood that he is able to go deeply into this way of engaging.

Ruby May is wonderful, isn't she?

Me and submission

As you can probably tell, I was more and more intrigued and inspired by BDSM and about the bits of me it shed light on.

But what of me being submissive? There was a lot sexually that I was practically tripping over myself to try, yet when it came to submission I was floundering. It just didn't hold the strength of desire and fantasy it used to, and I think there were a few issues at work here.

On the one hand, I was learning so much about how to facilitate my own pleasure and could now keep myself orgasming for as long as I wanted. I couldn't really imagine anyone else being able to give me more, or even as much, pleasure as I could give myself. I really liked having all this newly discovered mastery over my own sexual experience – it had taken me long enough to find, and now I was a bit reluctant to give it away. To stand naked before a man and say, 'You know better than me how to please me,' was actually what I had been doing unwittingly for years.

It made me think about something I had read of called the 'core erotic theme', in *The Erotic Mind* by Jack Morin. We all have a core erotic theme, apparently. It is that fantasy that will always turn us on, which when we look at it can actually often be traced back to the emotional climate we encountered when we were young.

When it came to my own core erotic theme thingummy, my fantasies used to be about me being dominated. Golly, I haven't really mentioned my fantasies to you, have I, which is rather strange, as we've been here for hours and you know practically everything else about me. But perhaps I haven't gone on about my fantasies because I seemed to have more fantasies before I started using porn regularly . . . and we started at porn really, didn't we.

Back in earlier days, most of my fantasies had me and/or other women being dominated. If I think about it, the women were admired, desired and dominated. In one fantasy, I was tied to a chair, I was in underwear, a man was opposite me, I think he was clothed, and two women stood either side of me. The man was commanding the women to undress me and arouse me. Some fantasies had a whole room full of young women being appraised and educated about sex by men who were clothed.

That definitely makes sense when I think back to the 'emotional climate' of my formative years, which was all Page 3, Benny Hill and films like *Screwballs*.

I wondered whether, because I'd been unpicking all of this stuff, I had shifted my core erotic theme so it no longer held the same power over me. What was my main fantasy now? I used much less fantasy than I had previously, but I did sometimes, when making love, imagine that Bell Tent Man was making love to someone else. If my erotic theme was my partner pleasuring another woman or women, was this because there was some unfinished emotional business relating to the openness of our relationship? Well, that could definitely be the case, as the reality of Bell Tent Man being with other women had at times caused me a fair bit of pain and brainache. Oh my goodness, I found this sex malarkey endlessly fascinating.

But I was curious to discover if actually experiencing sensual domination would reignite and excite my early erotic fantasies. And yet, I was stuck when it came to actually arranging it. There was something about the transaction of the sensual domination session that I was finding uncomfortable. What I really wanted was to go to a professional and pay him/her/them to give me the session I had in mind. The transaction would have been clear. I would be paying money to receive the experience I desired. However, I couldn't find anyone who offered this who wasn't in Sydney (or somewhere else equally distant) and anyway, there wasn't much money in the old bankeroony at the time. And even if I had found someone affordable who I felt comfortable with and who was in this country, I'm not sure how Bell Tent Man would have reacted to me going to see them.

This all meant that really Bell Tent Man was the only person who could play the dominant and make this session work for me. But it felt like such a BIG ask, monumental. 'Oh, can you just give me this amazing session where you just totally concentrate on making me come loads?' I wasn't quite going to put it like that, but I still found myself reticent about making the request. I was worried that he wouldn't enjoy the session.

Planning my submission session

As I was pondering all these issues, I came across a fella called DominantSoul during one of my internet trawls. He has a blog all about sensual domination, and I found the way he writes about it very helpful in terms of setting up my own experience with Bell Tent Man. In particular, he's written a whole blog post about how he structures his sensual domination sessions.[4] I've distilled a bit for you below. Huge thanks to DominantSoul for allowing me to quote it here.

The build-up: DominantSoul says he doesn't let his submissive touch herself for a week before their encounter. He gets her to plan a sexy outfit for the session, and then he flirts loads with her by text and email 'to keep her wet and distracted at work'. This, he says, ensures 'her mind and body are thoroughly aroused for many days before I ever touch her'. Right, yes, I'll have some of this build-up stuff, please.

Foreplay: 'A woman is like a sexual slow cooker,' says DominantSoul, and you have to slowly bring her 'to a steady boil to eventually make her overheat'. As part of his foreplay, he does lingerie modelling photoshoots with his submissives. I'm sorry, come again? Lingerie modelling! I couldn't think of anything worse. I bloody hate having my photo taken. I'd end up pulling my comedy gurning face, especially modelling my old pants.

I wondered what would get me feeling in the mood. Ooo, I know! There is a film called *Bliss*, where Terence Stamp plays a sex therapist who helps this young couple sort out their sex lives. He is a bit of a dude, very into conscious sexuality and sacred spots. He tells the guy in the film to touch his partner all over her body with the lightest of touches. I think I would like that, maybe administered with a feather – check me out. Props! I think I had better be blindfolded, as I think it will help me submit.

DominantSoul also says he uses certain acts to get his submissive feeling submissivey – hair pulling, talking deep and slow, a hand on her throat, throat fucking. Yes, I imagine that a spot of hair pulling and a penis in the mouth would make me feel submissive.

Right, the session is shaping up. Onwards!

Orgasm training: DominantSoul likes to play with different types of orgasm. 'There are many ways a woman can have an orgasm (vaginal, clitoral, G-spot, anal, breast, spanking, mind-gasms), so I will choose one or several of these to focus on during a session. I always want my submissive to experience numerous and multiple orgasms (more than ten) during a session,' he says. Golly, I think I would love G-spot, deep spot, clitoris and breast. (I feel like I'm ordering lunch suddenly.) You're not allowed to come until he says so, apparently. Bossy.

Subspace training: Now, he explains this as 'pushing her pain tolerance after multiple orgasms'. It's where I start to go, 'Oh, no pain, please!' But then again, I've been quite enjoying some impact play. So yes, I think I'd like a bit of spanking and flogging here.

Intercourse: DominantSoul describes this as the part where you 'reconnect intimately as a dom/sub'. He also says this is where,

'I want to fuck her literally into oblivion.' It's the fucking bit basically. I'll have some of that too.

Sensual aftercare: He likes to reward his women afterwards either with 'a full-body oil massage to soothe her exhausted body' or by 'holding her naked body for hours. It is the emotional connection a submissive craves after giving her body to such sexual extreme treatments.' Well, I'm always up for an oily massage and I generally love a nice cuddle, so I'd happily accept that.

My session

So I sent a lot of information, along with a link to Dominant-Soul's site, to Bell Tent Man to see if he might be able to do this session with me. It felt like a MASSIVE ask but he said yes, which I felt very grateful for. We scheduled it for two weeks' time, giving us lots of time for the build-up bit.

I have to admit that we were a bit shit at doing the sexy messages beforehand. But bless him, he went to town with the actual session. I was blindfolded and led into a room he had prepared beforehand. My senses were activated as he fed me little bits of fruit and chocolate, with music on in the background. I felt a feather run over my skin. But if I'm honest, I found it a bit hard to let go and relax; perhaps I was a bit more wary than aroused. Also, when Christian Grey is dominating whatsherchops in *Fifty Shades*, they are in a well-equipped and huge great dungeon, while we were in quite a small bedroom, banging into furniture and tripping over a towel that had been left on the floor.

I was fully naked and he manoeuvred me onto all fours with my bum in the air. Then he ordered me to part my bottom cheeks with my hands. OK, I have to step aside for a moment to shriek I FEEL REALLY ICKY AND ASHAMED WRITING THIS!!!! What is going on? I am a grown woman who had consented to a session with a partner I loved and trusted, and he had manoeuvred me into a position that made fingering my bum easy. It doesn't really warrant the mortification I felt then, or in fact, the mortification I am feeling now.

Anyway, he lightly touched my anus, and well, blimey, it was the sweetest, gentlest feeling. It felt as though it was calming me in a way I hadn't experienced before. But then his finger started to go inside and it felt like everything was crashing down for me. I felt panicky. I wanted it to stop. I waited for one long uncomfortable minute and then I ended the session. All I wanted was to be on my own, curled into a ball, on the sofa, in my onesie, which is what I did.

As I lay there, I remembered being caught on the floor with my knickers down when I was eight. Was all this anus angst because of that? What was going on?

Bums!

But arses weren't on the list, I hear you cry. I didn't sign up for bum stuff. Oh, I know, love, I know. Neither did I . . .

The thing you most resist

I met a really awesome woman at the 'In Love and Service' workshop who said something that struck me. And not just the one strike: it kept on jabbing.

She explained that her journey into BDSM started when she was messaged something kinky by someone on a dating site. She was about to send a 'Fuck off, pervert' response, when she thought, 'Hang on, that's a bit of a strong response, let's just lift this rock up, shall we, and see what's going on under here.' Four hours of messaging later, she said, and she was more turned on she had ever been in her life.

It was a bit of the old 'what you resist persists'. I asked myself, 'What am I resisting?' and the answer lunged at me. Bum stuff. Oh jeez, I was really resisting bum stuff. I'd never had anal sex, I'd endured only the very rare and incredibly brief bit of bum licking. Other people's anuses didn't bother me so much, but my own, well, I would much prefer that area just not to be included in the whole sex thing. Hmmm, the more I thought about it, the more I realised that I'd gone on a whole, 'love your body' jag and totally missed out my anus. Oh, my poor anus. Except I didn't feel sorry for it, I felt repulsed by it. I also realised that every single other person in the world had had anal sex except me, which meant that I was weird and repressed.

Oh, can't I put the rock back?!

Anal sex and me

So, anal sex. Over the years a few guys had tried, and I always said no. I had been scared in my twenties by witnessing someone over a few days go from, 'I love anal sex, I'm having loads of it,' to, 'I can't sit down,' to, 'Do I look yellow to you? I think I have to go to A&E.' Also, for me, it was about the fact that I shat from my arse. And I had some fairly unpleasant shit stories, including dysentery at eighteen while travelling causing me to poop myself on the street in Central America and other jolly tales. Ah, we know each other so well now.

Basically, when I thought about my arse I wasn't thinking, 'Sex me up, baby,' I was thinking, 'Stay away from it and let's pretend it isn't there.' I didn't want anyone to go near it, because if they did then that someone would literally be in my shit. WHY WOULD THEY WANT TO DO THAT? It seemed like THE most personal and exposing thing. It wasn't even an area I had explored myself. I just didn't want to.

But tender touch had been so life-changing when it came to my vulva and vagina that I started to feel that that if I turned attention to my anus in the same way something quite transformative might happen. Was this the place where my civilised, socialised self met the flesh-and-blood animal that I really am? What was I so afraid of?

Tender touch on the anus

A few days after our session Bell Tent Man and I spoke about how I had stopped the submission session after he touched my anus. Obviously, something was going on for me when it came to my bum area. We arranged a session where he would just very gently touch around and maybe in my anus, no pressure for sex or any outcome, just a 'shall we have a little relaxed bit of tender touch in that area and see what happens?' So we did, and again, ah, the touch on and around my anus, it was as though it was undoing a knot in my head that I hadn't realised had been keeping me all tight and tense for as long as I could remember. Even writing about it now I can feel a similar sensation of release. But when the finger moved and started to go inside, I crunched tight again and I had that same feeling of just wanting to curl up and hide, watch telly, zone out, and not talk to anyone, which is what I did.

But . . . and this is odd. The next day, when I woke, I felt as though I had slept really deeply for the first time in ages, and I was quite, well, it sounds weird, but *happy*. I can struggle a bit in the mornings and at that time I was a bit run down. The day after the tender-touch anus session I felt completely different to how I had been feeling for the previous week. This feeling carried on all day.

Now this made total sense when I read the Jack Morin bum book, more commonly referred to as *Anal Pleasure and Health*. In it, he says that the anus can be a chronic tension zone. It actually tenses up when you are stressed and can hold on to anxieties from way back.

Oh my goodness, maybe by finally focusing on this beleaguered area I was starting to say goodbye to some of this pent-up tension.

The next thing we did was an exercise from the Jack Morin book where you examine your anus with a mirror.

We used one of those moveable bathroom mirrors that magnifies everything, great for squeezing spots and dealing with a monobrow, interesting when it comes to looking at your fanny. So there we were, looking at my MASSIVE minge, and you would think it would be traumatic, but actually I found it fascinating and rather lovely. I hadn't been down there with a mirror since the days of learning how to insert a tampon.

'Hi, vulva, it's so nice to see you,' I said.

I'd learned to love my womanly bits because of how amazing they felt, but actually seeing it all was like greeting an old friend – admittedly a friend who had been through quite a lot. The whole area was fascinating. And then we came to my MASSIVE ANUS and, well, I wanted to give it a hug. I felt very tender towards it.

Another time we did an exercise known in sexual-healing circles as mapping, where you gently touch an area and say where it is you are touching as you do so. Sexological bodyworkers use mapping in this way to reactivate areas that have developed amnesia and numbness from trauma. It is so simple yet very powerful, as just by touching an area and naming it someone can reconnect with and activate a place that might have been shut down to sensation for a long time. One technique used is where you imagine a certain area is a clock face, say the anus, with twelve o'clock being nearest your vagina. You can then use the clock to locate different spots in the same region. We tried this and I had no clue where his finger was for the entirety of the session.

'So you're saying that this bit is six o'clock.' He took his finger away and then placed it on the same spot again. 'This bit . . . this bit . . . you're sure?' Bell Tent Man said to me, his finger touching two o'clock. I was unable to locate anywhere he was touching. It was as though the whole area had been in lockdown.

I am still on a very slow journey towards getting to know my bum. I think it is relaxing me generally. Also, I now like my anus being touched; it's the sort of arousing tingle I experience when my neck is caressed, only slightly more pleasurable. Good old Jack Morin suggests a finger up the bum for a minute or so while showering every day for optimum anal health and access to pleasure. I'm having a go at that too.

I've still not had anal sex. Yet. I may do. I have no burning desire to at the moment, although I have enjoyed a finger up my bottom while orgasming, so at some point it might seem like a natural end to this period of bum school. I could imagine taking it very slowly and almost ritualistically with my partner.

Kim Anami, sex and relationship expert, vaginal weight lifter and surfer (yes, you did read that right, awesome, eh?!) says of anal sex, 'There's plenty of information out there on how. (In short: lots of lube and go slow . . .) Very few people ever talk about why: it's cathartic and transformative.'[5] And I could imagine this to be true. But it's not a particularly strong pull just yet. I definitely don't feel horrified or scared at the thought any more though. I have made peace with an area of my body and that alone gives me options and freedom.

I am very glad I lifted the rock up.

AND THEN IT ALL CHANGED

Not ejaculating

As we bobbed around workshops during our summer of sexy love I noticed a lot of talk about something called the 21-Day Challenge. Mainly amongst the guys.

'Have you done the twenty-one day?'

'Yeah, struggled. Didn't get past eleven days. You?'

'Yeah, it's tough, man. I'm on day ninety-four.'

'DAY NINETY-FOUR!! Without ejaculating?! How are you feeling?'

'Goooood.'

'Hats off to you, bro.'

A chap called Alex Vartman had created this thing called the Advanced Sex™ 21-Day Challenge (sounds a bit like it was named by the Gillette razor-naming guys). He encourages men to go for twenty-one days without ejaculating and for women to go for twenty-one days without having a clitoral orgasm. He claims that most of us are in a post-orgasm fug, as after orgasm you experience a seventeen-day orgasm hangover, which depletes you of desire and energy.

Now, this is not a particularly new concept. The sexual

teachings of Taoism say that when a man ejaculates he becomes depleted, losing his vital life energy, and therefore in order to stay healthy, strong and youthful, he needs to knock ejaculation more or less on the head. (Although the Taoist teachings also claim that when women have sexual intercourse they age, so instead they should give blowjobs and use the semen as a face mask – the Taoists have some interesting views about semen.)

Bell Tent Man attempted the 21-Day Challenge about five months or so into our relationship. It was an odd period in time where every ejaculation would be followed by the gasped words, 'Bugger, bugger, shit, bugger.'

He did, in the end, rather brilliantly, master orgasming without ejaculation. He became a big fan of it, noting how drained of energy he felt when he did ejaculate in comparison to when he didn't. I noted how hard the sperm works when it is eventually released into the vagina, as it was at this time that he impregnated me.

Yes, you did read that correctly. Super-cool, busy, open, sexual-adventuring couple were having a baby.

I'm having a baby!

I hadn't originally intended to write about the impact having a baby had on my sexuality. The idea of this book came before I fell pregnant and I definitely hadn't spied a baby on the horizon. But in many ways another story about my sexuality starts with childbirth and it seems relevant to share at least a little bit of it.

I fell pregnant and it was wonderful. I felt as though I had been given the best job in the world. The only trouble was that I saw myself as the worst candidate for it. My life was not at all set up for babies. I wasn't earning, for a start. My finances had long been in a pickle. I had been campaigning for years, and as anyone who has campaigned will probably agree, when you are fuelled by a passion for a campaign you don't just put aside your own basic needs, you hurl them into the wrong skip at the dump. So I had no money, and I was living on toast, coffee and fags. Not only that, but I was living in a child-free house share and I was in an open relationship with someone I hadn't known that long. How could I/we bring up a baby? It was a lot to process, especially while constantly feeling as though I was dreadfully hungover on a boat in a storm. Although if all this was a shock for me, spare a thought for Bell Tent Man.

But we did it. We became expectant parents. This wasn't like the movies; there was no montage to music of us decorating a nursery while I became steadily bigger. Rather, we moved in with my parents and amassed as much hand-me-down gear as we could. But we were happy, in love, and when it came to sex, well, once I had been assured that penetration couldn't hurt the little one, I could not get enough of it.

And then there was the birth. Cor blimey. Well, if you are not au fait with birth, consider the size of a baby's head and imagine that coming out of a very small hole in between your legs. Yes, indeed. Ouch. I don't think my birth experience was particularly grisly when I compare it to other women's stories. A twelve-hour labour at home (well, at someone else's home – not really ideal, looking back on it) ending in a fifteen-mile blue-light ambulance ride along bumpy country lanes. A quick ventouse delivery where my vagina was cut and stitched, and the arrival of a healthy, perfect baby boy.

After the birth, I felt physically and emotionally traumatised. I couldn't sit down. I didn't sleep for a week. I remember wondering, as I sat on a rubber ring, if I'd ever feel my own vitality again. I felt a lot of shame at being so weak. I was supposed to have an orgasmic home birth, complete with Native American flute music and be up for a scenic walk the next day.

In those early days, I marvelled at Bell Tent Man. He was amazing with our baby, and he had been such a support during the birth. We were a beautiful team. Obviously, we couldn't have sex, but I would share his masturbation, we would kiss and I would feel arousal from his arousal. I remember so looking forward to when we could make love again.

Erm, we seem to have stopped having sex

But months and months later we still weren't having sex. And this felt like a big deal. Sex was what we did, for goodness' sake, it was our thing. I desperately wanted to revive that side of our connection but it felt really, really difficult to do so.

There seemed to be a few things at play. One was the tiredness, the absolute 'I can't be arsed'-ness, the 'I can barely get off the sofa and roll into bed, let alone ride us to bliss'-ness. What I found again and again was that although at various times in the daytime I would think, 'YES! I want to have sex tonight!' by the time night-time came and sex was on the table, I was so zonked that I just wanted to flop in front of the tellybox. Bell Tent Man seemed to be the same. It felt like a massive hurdle to get from that stuck-to-the-sofa fug to a place where sex could be even on the cards, a monumental and unfathomable leap to go from being two people who talked about recycling and nappy absorbency to two people who wanted to devour each other's naked bodies. We used to come to each other with passion; now we flopped and lolloped across the bed for a half-arsed kiss. Sex before had felt energetic; now it seemed lacklustre. Humph.

Oh, and penetration was either numb or uncomfortable and painful, even over seven months later. It could generally only be accomplished by me holding my breath, clenching my teeth and quietly panting the word 'fuuuuuck'.

My fear was that if I didn't do something different here, this situation would carry on and on. *If you always do what you have always done, you'll always get what you've always got.* So there I was, yet again starting over, and again asking, 'What do I want in relation to sex?'

The answer was strong and clear this time, and quite surprising. Though in retrospect I don't know why I was surprised, because again the first thing that sprung to my mind was that I wanted really slow sex. And interestingly, every woman who has read early drafts of this book has told me that when they think about it the number-one thing they want is also to experience really slow sex.

Yes, what I wanted was to be slowly, so fucking slowly, penetrated, and to be able to cry every step of the way. I wanted to feel that it was OK for the trauma in my body to be released. I didn't want to have to stick to a routine, or to perform, or to be something I used to be. I wanted to be made love to. I wanted to be touched tenderly, as though I was precious.

But all that was a pretty tall order for Bell Tent Man, who had enough of his own stuff going on. He was tired too and in shock at becoming a dad and all that it entails. I imagined us being in bed and me asking for what I wanted:

'Please touch me as though I am precious.'

He starts to touch me.

'Can you touch me as though I am really precious.'

'I am.'

'Really touch me tenderly, as though you love me and I am precious.'

'But I am.'

'I don't feel as though you are.'

'Well, I am doing the best I can.'

It's depressing and disempowering to pin all your needs on someone else. No, if I wanted to be touched tenderly, I could do that for myself. And so I made a pact to have a few of the old smelly-candle tantric wanks. Only I didn't really wank as such. Often I would just lie, and gently stroke my body all over, and then simply hold a hand lightly over my sex area and breathe. More often than not I would cry a little.

The more I thought about it, the more I realised that my sexuality had shifted quite dramatically, since I'd given birth. I wondered why I hadn't really acknowledged it until then. I used to watch porn fairly regularly and could generally find something to turn me on. Post-birth I didn't want to go near porn. I felt very strongly that I didn't want to go into the world of the big free porn sites. It sounds a bit dramatic, but I sensed that the oxytocin haze of early motherhood would somehow be 'contaminated' (that is the word that came to me). No, I didn't want porn anywhere near me, or the baby. This might be because what I wanted most of all was to be treated very tenderly – and I would hazard a guess that the word 'tenderness' has rarely, if ever, been used in association with online porn. Also, I didn't want the relationship to be open. Actually, scrap that: I couldn't handle the relationship being open. It became so important to me that we battened down the hatches at this time and concentrated on ourselves and this new family we had started. So this was what we eventually did.

In need of a shake-up

Alongside this, I thought about how Bell Tent Man and I were coming together sexually and about how lacking in energy we were. 'We need shaking up,' I thought. 'Hmmm, maybe we actually literally need shaking up.' Could I ask Bell Tent Man to jump around for a bit before we have sex?

'Er, babe, can we just jump around for a minute or two before we make out? I can put some music on. "Gangnam Style"?'

It was a bit whacky. But then again, why not? It had to be better than the lollop. And one thing I was fairly sure about was that Bell Tent Man enjoyed sex and would do anything, even if it did seem a little oddball, to get this side of things back on track.

But once I had convinced myself that it was OK to instigate dancing to bad South Korean pop before sex, I thought, 'Why stop there? We could do other stuff!' I searched online under headings like 'quick effective intimacy exercises'. Before I knew it, I had created a something called the Twenty-Minute Turnaround, which was twenty minutes of exercises to get us off the sofa and connected. There was dancing and hugging and uninterrupted talking, then looking into each other's eyes. I would just have to put it to him in a 'What the hell! We have nothing to lose! It might just be a giggle' kind of way. He already knew stuff was going on, because I kept lighting smelly candles and popping off for tantric wanks. And I felt better just from taking these little steps. It reminded me of an old quote I used to have written on a notebook: 'Worry disappears in the face of action.' And I felt quite pleased with myself. I don't think the old passive Lucy would have done this sort of thing.

Twenty-Minute Turnaround

1. **Three minutes – Dancing/shaking:** you know how you stir a pot or shake a snow globe? Well, you need to activate and energise your own matter in the same way. So get off the sofa, put on something up-tempo, whether it's 'Gangnam Style' or a particularly crescendo-y Mozart number, and hurl your body around, dance or shake to it for three minutes.

2. **One minute – Stand still and look into each other's eyes:** weirdly you may feel more uncomfortable doing this than busting out your dance moves, but go with it. Look into each other's eyes – nervous giggles, smiles and 'eek' faces, it's all fine. Just hold the gaze.

3. **Two minutes – Standing cuddle:** ooo, it's lovely this one.

4. **Three minutes each – Sharing with the other how you are feeling:** uh oh, I've mentioned feelings! This is probably the bit that is likely to scare people the most, but it's also the bit that will be the most profound. Three minutes of talking without being interrupted by your partner is often rather lovely. So, one person stands still and silent while the other one explores how they are feeling in that moment. 'I'm nervous doing this. I feel all young and school-girly,' 'I still feel a bit thrown that I got so angry with Lottie when she wouldn't go to bed,' 'I feel a bit butterflies-in-the-tummy to be doing this with you' etc., etc. The person listening just listens: no comments, no fidgets, no trying to check their Facebook messages or pull an ingrowing hair out of their neck. Just listening. Then swap.

5. **Four minutes each – The pleasure zone:** asking for touch from your partner. Taking it in turns, one person stands, sits or lies down and asks to be touched in a certain way or place. Whatever they want! 'Can you make your touch light like a feather and, starting on my face and neck, touch me all over?' Or, 'Can you massage my bum quite hard?' Whatever you fancy, ask, and if you'd like it harder, softer, or in a different place, gently say, 'Could you add a bit more pressure?' When the four minutes is up, say thank you and swap.

And that is the Twenty-Minute Turnaround Now, those twenty minutes may be all you fancy, and afterwards you might just want to snuggle up for some TV-watching, or you may want to extend the touch session, or have a chat, or make love. In my experience, it does turn things around in twenty minutes, so you feel more in touch with your partner and your own sensuality. I hope it does the same for you.

We tried it out and it did the trick. We turned off the telly! We got naked! It completely upped our levels of sexual oomf. It became a regular thing and we would alternate who choreographed the session.

Tender touch to the rescue again

But we still had a problem. Penetration was still as comfortable and erotic as stuffing a Cumberland sausage up my nose.

So I went on the internet, where I found a fella called Mike Lousada, who has a whole section on his website about the hands-on healing he offers for after-birth trauma.[1] Blimey, I thought, as I emailed him for an appointment, I'm going to pay a man to play with my bits. Or perhaps not, I thought, when he emailed back to tell me a session would likely cost £700. Now, I reckon this would have been money well spent, if I'd had it, but I didn't, and even if we had had it, that would have been a family holiday.

However, I received some healing anyway. And not by Mike Lousada. Even better than that, it was by Bell Tent Man. And it wouldn't have happened if we hadn't done the Twenty-Minute Turnaround – a fact that really encourages me to keep coming up with outlandish suggestions.

So, yes, the Twenty-Minute Turnaround session quickly became routine. We alternated who choreographed each session, with Bell Tent Man nearly always joking 'a twenty-minute blowjob' when it was his turn to pick what we were doing. He never suggested any talking about feelings, but didn't seem to mind it when I did.

We were doing a session one evening when I asked for the tops of my thighs to be massaged. Quite often since the birth, if I really tuned in and thought about what I needed body-wise, it was a hard massage at the tops of my legs, inside and outside. I wonder whether it's anything to do with the last part of pregnancy when there was a big baby's head bearing down there. The tops of my legs really ached, especially at night. This wasn't so easy to do myself, so I had asked Bell Tent Man to help me.

Anyway, he was massaging the tops of my thighs and I was quite vocal about how it was affecting me, in a good way. Then, when my time was up, he said, 'What now?'

'Are you able to gently massage around the edge of my vagina?' I asked. I wanted to be ever so gently massaged around the whole of the base of my vulva. So he began. And I let out a big sigh. Within seconds, the gentlest of touches on the area where I had my stitches had me crying, images of my labour coming back to me. I didn't want him to move much, just to very gently keep his finger on this area.

Well, I cried and cried. And then when we'd finished, I lay there and the area carried on responding to a touch that wasn't there, and I continued to cry.

For me this was the most wonderful and healing experience. The question 'why didn't we do this before?' lingered unsaid. Once we'd begun, it seemed so obvious that this was what was needed. We started to do this regularly, including touch up and inside the vagina, and then, when it felt right, we tried consciously and incredibly slowly penetrating the vagina with his penis.

I think I'd tried to get back to super sex too quickly and simply bypassed reacquainting myself with this area. The area had been frozen, in shock, perhaps, and couldn't respond. But in this way, slowly and quite beautifully this area came to life again.

What I am realising is that when it comes to sexuality, the story never ends. There will always be major incidents to shake things up – next it could be menopause, or the impact of illness, the death of a loved one, relationship challenges. I guess I will always be transforming and coming back to a new beginning, hopefully a little wiser than before. Situations and events will always be rendering me, and my body, anew, and each time I'll have to come to know myself again. Who am I physically and emotionally now? And what is it I want and need at this time?

THE END OF THE BOOK

So here we are, pretty much at the end of this, my sex book.

I haven't made a porn film yet, I'm afraid. But there is a little something in the pipeline. A simple ninety-second film featuring women asking what they want in sexual situations. There is a lot of sex on the internet and we are used to the male voice commanding proceedings: 'Show me your pussy,' 'Bend over,' etc. In this film I'm making we only hear the woman asking for what she wants. It is a tiny antidote to what is currently on offer, a minuscule drop in the ocean of pornography. But I hope it will be powerful nonetheless.

It's hard to know how to end a book like this, possibly because as I've said, with sexuality there is no fixed end point. We're unlikely to land somewhere and live there harmoniously ever after as we're always morphing and changing, like those we are relating with and the world around us.

I definitely haven't found all the answers. But I do enjoy asking the questions. The main one being, 'When it comes to sex, what do I want?' and then allowing myself to ask the next one, 'Can I bring that into my life? And if so, how?' They are questions I wish, wish, wish I had started asking myself sooner. I feel sad at how much time I spent worrying about whether I was desirable instead of thinking about what I desired. For me, sexual empowerment wasn't found in fancy lingerie or learning to pole dance but in learning to say 'no', or, 'Could you touch me there a little gentler please.'

I have found such power in this, and also in greeting myself as a friend. I am simply Lucy, and I am fine as I am. I have characteristics and traits which, yes, can sometimes be a bit infuriating. I have done many, many things that I am not proud of or wish I had done better. I have physical features that might mean I'll never be a pin-up. But the sum of me, the gloriously complicated whole of me, is beautiful. I have a heart that loves fiercely and gets inspired regularly and I try. I am OK as I am.

And that alone might be the biggest gift that exploring my sexuality has given me. Because on this affection for myself, I can hang everything else. I remember when I was thinking about starting the campaign against Page 3, people said, 'But they will destroy you.' The *Sun* newspaper was known for dishing the dirt on people, bringing them down. An MP had stood up years before on the same subject and they had branded her 'fat and jealous'.[1] But I had felt destroyed before; the little girl, the woman, who hated herself and was ashamed of her looks, she had been pretty much destroyed already. And I didn't feel that anyone could destroy this sense of love and peace I now felt for myself, and so I was strong enough to stand up and speak out.

People come to this self-love in different ways. I came to it through sex, which I recommend as being a fun route. But I have to say that I found this route spiritual too.

There, I've said it. It's not a word we are that comfortable with in Britain, so I am almost wary of sharing it with you.

It was strange. I grew up with religions teaching me about celibacy, abstinence, 'saving myself' and notions of being damned or tainted if had sex for any reason other than to produce children. Yet journeying into my own physical pleasure, on my own and with others, seemed, more than anything, to make me feel that there was some sort higher power. And it wasn't saying, 'Don't do this,' it was saying, 'Welcome, what took you so long?'

I was doubting myself for talking about spirituality here, but it feels so apt to do so, if purely for the fact that for thousands of years man has ruled and punished female sexuality in the name of religion, in the name of God. We were supposed to worship God with pious lives of abstinence and apology. But what if God isn't a sexist bastard? What if he, or she, or they, gave us bodies capable of exquisite pleasure for us to enjoy, be grateful for, and use to bring us closer to them?

All through the writing of this book, I have had an awareness that I am free, but so many women alive now aren't, as so many women who went before me weren't. I've thought of my female ancestors, and how until really recently, they couldn't vote, or buy property. Until 1991 it was legal for a wife to be raped by her husband. Let's fucking well repeat that. Until 1991 a man could rape his wife in the UK (apparently an advanced, humane, developed country).

And, crikey, am I aware of, and deeply grateful for all the opportunities and privileges that have allowed me to sit here day after day and write a book about sex: for the education I had which means I can write and read, for the fact that I don't live as part of a society or religious community who will condemn, punish or kill me for having sex, or for speaking out about it. For my male partner, who doesn't feel that housework and childcare is my lot, but who encourages me and is looking after our child and maybe even making me breakfast at this very moment.

It is a strange one, writing a book about female sexuality and sharing as explicitly as I have. Oftentimes I've thought, 'Why am I doing this?' There is an ever-nagging sense that I will bring shame on people who love me, or I'll disappoint those who campaigned with me. But then I suppose that it is this very fact that we are just so weird when it comes to sex that keeps driving me. It feels like we're always talking about it, but never *really* talking about it. It's either innuendo, *nudge nudge, cor, I'd bang that*, or ban everything! I think we've been missing out on important discussions about how it actually makes us feel.

Anyway, if telling this story inspires just one young woman not to feel she has to compare herself to the images she sees in magazines, or take part in sex that she feels uncomfortable with, or if it inspires her to start a petition and challenge something that makes her feel small – well, if my story can do that, then I feel it is a story worth telling.

Somewhere along the line, we, women, forgot how powerful we are.

Let's not forget again.

A HERSTORY OF WOMEN AND SEX

2100 BCE

The Ancient Sumerians

The oldest written law we have still in existence is from the Sumerian kingdom of Ur-Nammu, and it stated that married women who seduced other men were to be killed, while their lovers were let off scot-free.[1]

1000 BCE

The Assyrians

Their law was clear that a husband could punish his wife by whipping and hitting her, pulling her hair, and mutilating her ears.[2]

These guys were really into women's virginity and had pretty intricate laws surrounding it. Things like, if an unmarried woman was raped, financial compensation was given to her father; he could also force the rapist to marry his daughter and also take the rapist's wife as a slave.[3]

Fuckadoodle, these ancient guys were psychotic. Still, at least we're moving into classical antiquity now with all those sage old thinkers and philosophers.

Ancient Greece

Aristotle, says in his work *Politics*: 'As regards the sexes, the male is by nature superior and the female inferior, the male ruler and the female subject.'

Yeah, but how influential could one beardy geezer be anyway??

'Aristotle's writings . . . have influenced virtually every avenue of human knowledge pursued in the west and the east.[4]

Bollocks.
   Still, these laws can't be as bad for women as the Assyrian and Sumerian laws. I mean, they were mental.

The ancient Greeks considered war rape of women 'socially acceptable behaviour well within the rules of warfare', and warriors considered the conquered women 'legitimate booty, useful as wives, concubines, slave labour, or battle-camp trophy'.[5]

What about the Romans? Surely they liked the ladies?

The Roman Code of Paterfamilias reads, 'If you should discover your wife in adultery, you may with impunity put her to death without a trial, but if you should commit adultery or indecency, she must not presume to lay a finger on you, nor does the law allow it.'[6]

Hang about! I bet God didn't like all this. Peace and love and all that. What were the religious dudes saying?

'To the woman [God] said, I will make your pains in childbearing very severe; with painful labour you will give birth to children. Your desire will be for your husband, and he will rule over you.' Genesis 3:16 (first book of the Hebrew Bible and Old Testament)

I don't know about you, sisters, but I'm having trouble spotting the love.

'If, however, the charge is true and no proof of the girl's virginity can be found, she shall be brought to the door of her father's house and there the men of her town shall stone her to death.' Deuteronomy 22:20–1

Guys, we need to have a word. Can you just lay off the murdering women? You're not to murder a woman for having sex, or potentially having had sex, do you get me, capiche? You have some acute anger and overreaction issues going on, and, I hate to say it, but you need to be like, kept away from people. You definitely shouldn't be making laws and creating religious rules, OK?

'If a man happens to meet a virgin who is not pledged to be married and rapes her and they are discovered, he shall pay her father fifty shekels of silver. He must marry the young woman, for he has violated her. He can never divorce her as long as he lives.' Deuteronomy 22:28–9

Who is making this shit up? Can I . . . helloooo . . . is anyone listening?
  What even is this Deuteronomy anyway?
  The fifth book of the Torah, also known as Jewish Written law, and a book in the Old Testament too.
  Fuckety fuck.
  No words.

But I know what happens now, Jesus rocks up, and everyone starts singing 'Kumbaya'.

Hmmmmmm.

Shit.

Sadly not, the religious dudes get really mental now. 150CE–500CE, *is the patristic age, as in the word 'pater' (meaning father) patriarch, patriarchy. This period was all about the 'Christian fathers' – men.*

I'll try to explain a bit about this. From what I can gather, the guys blamed the girls for pretty much everything because Eve ate an apple in the Garden of Eden. (Er, that's a myth, guys, it's like panto! It's not true!) And then apparently the Son of God had to die to cleanse us of the apple-eating sin. So Jesus dying was women's fault.

Oookay, so what were these beardy thinkers saying about us now?

- 'You *are the devil's gateway:*
- *you are the unsealer of that (forbidden) tree:*
- *you are the first deserter of the divine law:*
- *you are she who persuaded him (Adam) whom the devil was not valiant enough to attack.*
- You *destroyed so easily God's image, man.*
- *On account of* your *desert – that is, death – even the Son of God had to die.'*[7]

Tertullian, from *De Cultu Feminarum*,
book 1, chapter 1

Ouchie! Who is this nutter? I bet he's been hailed as Psycho Tulli. Nope, 'the father of Latin Christianity' and 'the founder of Western theology'.[8] *Oh wow, you couldn't make this shit up.*

So, early Christianity and Judaism, which you would have hoped and expected to be about loving each other, weren't so kind to the ladies. How about the other religions? Shall we have a peek?

Quran

'Men are in charge of women by [right of] what Allah has given one over the other and what they spend [for maintenance] from their wealth. So righteous women are devoutly obedient, guarding in [the husband's] absence what Allah would have them guard. But those [wives] from whom you fear arrogance – [first] advise them; [then if they persist], forsake them in bed; and [finally], strike them. But if they obey you [once more], seek no means against them. Indeed, Allah is ever Exalted and Grand.'[9]

Hinduism

'[When creating them] Manu allotted to women [a love of their] bed, [of their] seat and [of] ornament, impure desires, wrath, dishonesty, malice, and bad conduct.' *Manusmriti*, 9.17 [10]

Buddhism

According to the Vinaya and other early scriptures, the Buddha originally refused to ordain women as nuns. He said that allowing women into the *sangha* would cause his teachings to survive only half as long – 500 years instead of 1,000.[11]

Shit, even the Buddhists!

Why did I get into religion, it's a bloomin' nightmare.

There's a Christian reformation period coming up, isn't there? This must be when the guys get together and apologise for religion perpetuating the abuse of women for thousands of years. Yeah, and then they make sure that women are educated,

230 DON'T HOLD MY HEAD DOWN

so they can start writing their own histories and shaping the world . . . Yee ha!

'Women are not created for any other purpose than to serve man and to be his assistant in producing children.'[12]
Martin Luther, reformer (1483–1546)

Oh please . . . when do we get to the happy ending?

1700–1800s

'White men perpetrated millions of rapes against women of colour. All of them, by greater or lesser degrees, confirmed sex as racial and cultural domination.'[13]

I am weeping now.
    But there is more . . . and more and more . . . women killed for being 'witches', families murdering their daughters and sisters and calling it 'honour', female genital cutting, child brides.
    And how is it all looking now?
    Well:

Sexual violence is still very much used in warfare.

'In Rwanda, between 100,000 and 250,000 women were raped during the three months of genocide in 1994.
    'UN agencies estimate that more than 60,000 women were raped during the civil war in Sierra Leone (1991–2002), more than 40,000 in Liberia (1989–2003), up to 60,000 in the former Yugoslavia (1992–95), and at least 200,000 in the Democratic Republic of the Congo since 1998.'[14]

But it isn't just in warfare; violence against women is, to quote the leader of the World Health Organisation (WHO), Margaret Chan, 'a global problem of epidemic proportions'.[15]

World Health Organisation statistics (as of November 2016):[16]

- Global estimates published by WHO indicate that about one in three (35 per cent) of women worldwide have experienced either physical and/or sexual intimate partner violence or non-partner sexual violence in their lifetime.
- Most of this violence is intimate partner violence. Worldwide, almost one third (30 per cent) of women who have been in a relationship report that they have experienced some form of physical and/or sexual violence by their intimate partner in their lifetime.
- Globally, as many as 38 per cent of murders of women are committed by a male intimate partner.

Around the world, 603 million women live in countries where domestic violence is not considered a crime and more than 2.6 billion live in countries where marital rape is not a criminal offence (figure from 2011).[17]

Estimates say there are 200 million girls and woman living with FGM (female genital mutilation).[18]

One child bride is married every seven seconds.[19]

Of the 774 million adults (fifteen years and older) who still cannot read or write, two thirds of them (493 million) are women. More than 60 per cent of adult women in Arab states, south and west Asia, and sub-Saharan Africa are still illiterate.[2]

But.

And there is a but.

Thank goodness.

We are witnessing something else.

An uprising.

A revolution.

And I don't know about you, but I can feel it gathering pace.

For the last hundred years or so, thanks to the hard work of women (and their male allies) campaigning, a tide has been steadily turning.

There is progress.

Even if it feels agonisingly slow.

1890–2017

1893 New Zealand is the first country to recognise women's right to vote.[21]

1911 The first ever International Women's Day is celebrated.[22]

1913 Marie Curie is awarded the Nobel Prize for Chemistry.[23]

1918 Russian women strike for 'bread for peace'.[24]

1918 Universities in Thailand open to women.[25]

1920 The USA grants women the right to vote.[26]

1920 Nepal: Sati is banned (practice where a widow takes her own life after her husband dies).[27]

1922 Iraq admits its first female student to university.[28]

1922 Syria: Muslim women appear unveiled for the first time in public.[29]

1928 All British women achieve the same voting rights as men.[30]

1934 Brazil and Thailand grant women the right to vote.[31]

1945 Indonesia grants women the right to vote.[32]

1947 Pakistan grants women the right to vote.[33]

1949 China grants women the right to vote.[34]

1950 India grants women the right to vote.[35]

1960 The FDA (Food and Drug Administration) in the USA

approves the world's first commercially produced birth control pill.[36]

1970 The Equal Pay Act is passed in the UK.[37]

1971 The first unofficial refuge for domestic-violence survivors opens in Hounslow, UK.[38]

1974 The National Women's Aid Federation is established, linking groups from England, Scotland and Wales to clarify the goals for developing shelter and services for women fleeing violence.[39]

1975 World Conference on Women, is held between 19 June and 2 July in Mexico City, Mexico. It was the first international conference held by the United Nations to focus solely on women's issues and marked a turning point in policy directives.[40]

1980 President Vigdís Finnbogadóttir of Iceland becomes the world's first democratically elected female president.[41]

1991 Rape in marriage is made illegal in the UK.[42]

1994 All South African women are allowed to vote.[43]

1997 Marital rape is criminalised in Germany.[44]

2006 Ellen Johnson Sirleaf becomes President of Liberia, the first elected female head of state in Africa.[45]

2007 FGM is banned in Egypt.[46]

2011 UN Women formed to further the empowerment of women and girls.[47]

2011 Women in Saudi Arabia are granted the right to vote.[48]

2012 Everyday Sexism project is founded by Laura Bates – it becomes a worldwide movement calling out sexism.[49]

2014 The Council of Europe Convention on preventing and combating violence against women and domestic violence (known as the Istanbul Convention), becomes the first legally binding instrument in Europe in the field of domestic violence and violence against women, which creates obligations on states that choose to ratify it.[50]

2014 Malala Yousafzai, Pakistani activist for girls' education, wins the Nobel Peace Prize.[51]

2015 Gambia and Nigeria ban FGM.[52]

2015 The *Sun* newspaper stops showing Page 3 pictures of topless young women, which it had been doing for forty-five years in the UK.[53] (Well, I had to put this one in, didn't I? #wedidit)

2017 Women in Saudi Arabia are allowed to drive.[54]

2017 #MeToo movement explodes onto social media as, in the wake of the Harvey Weinstein scandal, thousands of women share their experiences of sexual assault and harassment, saying, 'Me too.'[55]

2017 Merriam-Webster declares 'feminism' the word of the year. Today's Merriam-Webster definition of feminism reads: 'the theory of the political, economic, and social equality of the sexes' and 'organized activity on behalf of women's rights and interests'.[56]

Each of these rights came about because of individuals demanding them.

Thanks go to those dear sisters, alive and dead, for their protest.

But.

I'm sorry, this time, that there is a but.

The fact remains that the statistics of inequality and of violence against women are shocking and shameful.

And remember that for each statistic there is a woman or a girl, a daughter, a sister, a mother, a friend, a life ended in terror or lived in fear, potential diminished.

Sadly, we are talking lifetimes of effort to change lives on the scale we need.

So today I challenge myself.

What more can I do?

Because I can do more.

I can donate. I will make sure that going forward a percentage of what I earn goes towards helping women and girls and achieving equality.

I can volunteer. I will offer at least two hours a week of my time to support a local women's charity. If they don't need me I can use this time to help campaigns I care about.

I can write. Now this book is finished I will begin writing about male violence in all its forms, trying to fathom how we ended up living in such a violent world and asking what we can do about it. Because on some days this is all I think about and because when I write, I process, and it is then I take action.

And now I leave you with the challenge.

What more can you do?

Xx

Endnotes

1 Family Lives, under 'Pornography' at https://www.familylives.
   org.uk/advice/secondary/online/pornography/ on 29/05/18
2 Mail Online, News, under 'Three-quarters of teachers fear
   easy access to hardcore porn through smartphones and web
   is "damaging" pupils' at http://www.dailymail.co.uk/news/
   article-2223530/Three-quarters-teachers-fear-easy-access-
   hardcore-porn-smartphones-web-damaging-pupils.html   on
   29/05/18
3 politics.co.uk, Comment and Analysis, under 'David
   Cameron's porn speech in full', at http://www.politics.co.uk/
   comment-analysis/2013/07/22/david-cameron-s-porn-speech-
   in-full on 29/05/18

SLOW SEX – A BUMPY START

1 Diamond Light Tantra, under 'The Truth About Tantric Sex'
   – *Real Magazine*, at http://diamondlighttantra.com/node/1744
   on 29/05/18

LEARNING TO LOVE MYSELF

1 Diana Richardson, *The Heart of Tantric Sex*, O Books, UK. 2003. Page 35

ORGASMS, PLEASURE AND POWER

1 The Richest, under 'Fabian Thylmann Net Worth', at https://www.therichest.com/celebnetworth/celebrity-business/tech-millionaire/fabian-thylmann-net-worth/ on 29/05/18

2 Kinsey Confidential, under 'Are you Curious about the Clitoris?' At https://kinseyconfidential.org/clitoris/ on 29/05/18

3 ResearchGate, under 'Anatomy of the Clitoris', at https://www.researchgate.net/publication/7616832_Anatomy_of_the_Clitoris on 29/05/18

4 HuffPost, under 'History, The Clitoris' Vanishing Act' at http://projects.huffingtonpost.com/projects/cliteracy/history (29/05/18)

5 Howstuffworks, under 'Clitoris – the only organ designed for pleasure' at https://health.howstuffworks.com/sexual-health/female-reproductive-system/clitoris-dictionary1.htm on 29/05/18

6 BBC News, Health, under 'Time for rethink on the clitoris' at http://news.bbc.co.uk/1/hi/5013866.stm on 29/05/18

7 Encyclopedia.com, under 'Female Genital Mutilation', at https://www.encyclopedia.com/social-sciences/encyclopedias-almanacs-transcripts-and-maps/female-genital-mutilation on 29/05/18

8 HuffPost, under 'The Clitoris Through the Years' at http://projects.huffingtonpost.com/projects/cliteracy/history on 29/05/18

9 Ibid.

10 Ibid.

11 Ibid.

12 Ibid.

13 World Health Organisation, Factsheets, under 'Female Genital Mutilation', at http://www.who.int/mediacentre/factsheets/fs241/en/ on 29/05/18

14 Medical Daily, under 'Italian Scientist Says G-spot Doesn't Exist', at http://www.medicaldaily.com/italian-scientist-says-g-spot-doesnt-exist-cuv-region-new-erogenous-zone-may-hold-key-300056 on 29/05/18

15 *Cosmopolitan*, under 'The Full Body Orgasm You've Never Heard Of' https://www.cosmopolitan.com/sex-love/advice/a6896/cervical-orgasm-guide/ on 29/05/18

16 Wiley Online Library, under 'Ejacualtion, female, Beverly Whipple' at http://onlinelibrary.wiley.com/doi/10.1002/9781118896877.wbiehs125/full on 29/05/18

17 *Vice*, under 'Hitting the A-Spot Feels so Good', at https://www.vice.com/en_us/article/434wxb/this-is-how-to-hit-the-other-g-spot-the-a-spot on 29/05/18

18 *Women's Health*, under 'Butt Orgasms Are REAL – Here's How to Have One', at https://www.womenshealthmag.com/sex-and-love/how-to-have-butt-orgasms on 29/05/18

19 ResearchGate, under 'Non-genital orgasms' at https://www.researchgate.net/publication/241739177_Non-genital_orgasms on 29/05/18

20 *Cosmopolitan*, under 'Types of female orgasm explained', at https://www.cosmopolitan.com/uk/love-sex/sex/a9653627/different-types-of-female-orgasm/ on 29/05/18

21 ResearchGate, under 'Non-genital orgasms' at https://www.researchgate.net/publication/241739177_Non-genital_orgasms on 29/05/18

22 Annie Sprinkle and Beth Stephens, *The Explorer's Guide to*

Planet Orgasm: For Everybody, Greenery Press (CA) 2017

23 Annie Sprinkle.org(asm) under 'Seven Types of Female Orgasm' at http://anniesprinkle.org/seven-types-of-female-orgasm/ on 28/05/18

24 *Cosmopolitan*, under The Full-Body Orgasm You've Never Heard Of, at https://www.cosmopolitan.com/sex-love/advice/a6896/cervical-orgasm-guide/ on 29/05/18

25 KW Coaching, The Elusive Female Orgasm, under 'Vaginal Orgasm', at https://www.tantrictransformation.com/tag/education-2/page/4/ on 29/05/18

26 Rapecrisis.org.uk, article no longer accessible

MEN'S BITS

1 Canadian Foreskin Awareness Project, under 'Penile frenulum orgasm ("fremgasm")' at (http://can-fap.net/preview/fundraiser_preview_fremgasm.shtml on 29/05/18

THE SUMMER OF SEX

1 The Summer House Weekend, under 'What does consent mean in practice at play parties', at https://thesummerhouseweekend.com/consent-in-practice on 29/05/18

2 BettyMartin.org,   bettymartin.org/download-wheel   on 28/09/18

BDSM

1 *Vice*, under 'The A–Z of Sexual History: S, the Marquis of Sade', at https://www.vice.com/en_uk/article/mvw45x/a-to-z-

of-sexual-history-s-is-for-the-marquis-de-sade-god-daddy-of-sadism on 29/05/18

2 Ruby Luna May, Alchemy & Eros, under 'In Love and Service', at http://www.alchemy-eros.com/in-love-service/ on 21/09/18

3 Ruby Luna May, Alchemy & Eros, under 'On Penetration', at http://www.alchemy-eros.com/on-penetration/ on 29/05/18

4 DominantSoul, the Erotic Art of Sensual Domination, under 'Sensual Domination Session Framework: A Recipe for Mind-Blowing Domination Sessions', at https://dominantsoul.wordpress.com/sensual-domination/sensual-domination-framework-a-recipe-for-mind-blowing-domination-sessions/ on 29/05/18

5 Kim Anami, blog, under 'How Anal Are You?' http://kimanami.com/how-anal-are-you/ on 29/05/18

AND THEN IT ALL CHANGED

1 Mike Lousada, Psychoexual Therapy & Bodywork in London, under 'Healing Birth Trauma', at https://www.mikelousada.com/20/Healing-Birthing-Trauma.html on 29/05/18

THE END OF THE BOOK

1 *Guardian*, Media, under 'Sun Turns on Killjoy Short in Page 3 row', at https://www.theguardian.com/media/2004/jan/14/pressandpublishing.politicsandthemedia on 29/05/18

A HERSTORY OF WOMEN AND SEX

1 Eric Berkowitz, *Sex & Punishment: 4000 Years of Judging Desire*, Westbourne Press, UK, 2013, page 19.

2 Ibid., page 31

3 Ibid., page 30

4 The Ancient History Encyclopedia, under 'Aristotle', at https://www.ancient.eu/aristotle/ on 29/05/18

5 Wikipedia under 'Wartime Sexual Violence', at https://en.wikipedia.org/wiki/Wartime_sexual_violence#Pre-modern_European_era on 29/05/18
  Primary source cited: *Askin, Kelly Dawn* (1997). War Crimes Against Women: Prosecution in International War Crimes Tribunals. Martinus Nijhoff Publishers. *ISBN* 90-411-0486-0.

6 WomenSafe under, 'Overview of Historical Laws that Supported Domestic Violence' at http://www.womensafe.net/home/index.php/domesticviolence/29-overview-of-historical-laws-that-supported-domestic-violence on 29/05/18

7 Women Can be Priests, under Tertullian, at www.womenpriests.org maintained by Wijngaards Institute for Catholic Research on 29/05/18

8 Wikipedia, under Tertullian, at https://en.wikipedia.org/wiki/Tertullian (29/05/18). Primary sources cited: Benham, William (1887), *The Dictionary of Religion*, p. 1013. Ekonomou, Andrew J. (2007), *Byzantine Rome and the Greek Popes: Eastern influences on Rome and the papacy from Gregory the Great to Zacharias, AD 590–752*. Lexington Books, page 22.
  Gonzáles, Justo L. (2010), *'The Early Church to the Dawn of the Reformation'*, *The Story of Christianity*. New York: HarperCollins Publishers, pages 91–93 on 29/05/18

9 Qur'an, Sahih Internation, under 'Surat An-Nisa (The Women)' at http://legacy.quran.com/4/34 on 29/05/18

10 Manusmriti in Sanskrit with English translation at https://
archive.org/stream/ManuSmriti_201601/Manu-Smriti#page/
n187/mode/2up on 29/05/18

11 Barbara O'Brien, 'Buddhism and Sexism', ThoughtCo, at
thoughtco.com/buddhism-and-sexism-449757 on 29/05/18

12 John McKeown, 'Martin Luther: Forerunner of Natalism?' in
*God's Babies: Natalism and Bible Interpretation in Modern
America* [online]. Cambridge: Open Book Publishers,
2014 (generated 29 May 2018). Available at: http://books.
openedition.org/obp/2340
Primary source cited: *Luther on Women: A Sourcebook*, eds.
Susan C. Karant-Nunn and Merry E. Wiesner. Cambridge:
Cambridge University Press, 2003, page 17

13 Berkowitz, op. cit., page 257

14 United Nations, under 'Background Information on Sexual
Violence used as a Tool for War', at http://www.un.org/en/
preventgenocide/rwanda/about/bgsexualviolence.shtml on
29/05/18

15 World Health Organisation under 'Violence Against Women:
a global health problem of epidemic proportions' at http://
www.who.int/mediacentre/news/releases/2013/violence_
against_women_20130620/en/ on 29/05/18

16 World Health Organisation, Factsheets, under 'Violence
Against Women', at http://www.who.int/mediacentre/
factsheets/fs239/en/ on 29/05/18

17 *Guardian*, Global Development, under 'UN Women Justice
report', at https://www.theguardian.com/global-development/
poverty-matters/2011/jul/06/un-women-legal-rights-data on
29/05/18

18 World Health Organisation, Factsheets, under 'FGM' at
http://www.who.int/mediacentre/factsheets/fs241/en/ on
29/05/18

19 BBC News, World, under 'Girl under 15 married every 7

seconds, says Save the Children' at http://www.bbc.co.uk/news/world-37614798 on 29/05/18

20 *Guardian*, Working in Development, under 'The Literacy Injustice: 493 million women still can't read' at https://www.theguardian.com/global-development-professionals-network/2014/jun/17/literacy-women-illiteracy-development on 29/05/18

21 Infoplease, under Women's Suffrage at https://www.infoplease.com/us/gender-sexuality/womens-suffrage on 29/05/18

22 United Nations Foundation, under 'Key Dates in International Women's History', at http://www.unfoundation.org/assets/pdf/key-dates-in-international-womens-history.pdf on 29/05/18

23 Ibid.

24 Ibid.

25 Wikipedia, under 'Timeline of Women's Legal Rights (other than voting)' primary source cited; Patit Paban Mishra, (2010), *The History of Thailand*. Greenwood Histories of the Modern Nations, ABC–CLIO, on 29/05/18

26 Infoplease, under Women's Suffrage at https://www.infoplease.com/us/gender-sexuality/womens-suffrage on 29/05/18

27 ThoughtCo, under 'What is Sati' at https://www.thoughtco.com/what-is-sati-195389 on 29/05/18

28 Wikipedia, under 'Timeline of Women's Legal Rights (other than voting)' primary source cited Rubin, Barry, ed. (2012), *The Middle East: A Guide to Politics, Economics, Society and Culture* on 29/05/18

29 Wikipedia, under 'Timeline of Women's Legal Rights (other than voting)' primary source cited *Colonial Citizens: Republican Rights, Paternal Privilege and Gender in French Syria and Lebanon*, Columbia University Press on 29/05/18

30 Infoplease, under 'Women's Suffrage' at https://www.infoplease.com/us/gender-sexuality/womens-suffrage on 29/05/18

31 United Nations Foundation, under 'Key Dates in International Women's History' http://www.unfoundation.org/assets/pdf/key-dates-in-international-womens-history.pdf on 29/05/18

32 Infoplease, under Women's Suffrage at https://www.infoplease.com/us/gender-sexuality/womens-suffrage on 29/05/18

33 Ibid.

34 Ibid.

35 Women's Suffrage and Beyond, under 'The Women's Suffrage Timeline' at http://womensuffrage.org/?page_id=69 on 29/05/18

36 FDA, under 'FDA's Approval of the First Oral Contraceptive', Enovid https://www.fda.gov/downloads/AboutFDA/WhatWeDo/History/ProductRegulation/UCM593499.pdf on 29/05/18

37 Manchester Metropolitan University, under https://www.mmu.ac.uk/equality-and-diversity/doc/gender-equality-timeline.pdf on 29/05/18

38 UN Women, under 'The history and origin of women's sheltering', at http://www.endvawnow.org/en/articles/1368-the-history-and-origin-of-womens-sheltering.html?next=1369 on 29/05/18

39 Ibid.

40 UN Women, under 'World Conference of the International Women's Year', at http://www.un.org/womenwatch/daw/beijing/mexico.html on 29/05/18

41 Worldwide Guide to Women in Leadership, under 'Presidents', at http://www.guide2womenleaders.com/Presidents.htm on 29/05/18

42 Rights of Women, under 'Sexual Violence, Make it a Crime campaign', at http://rightsofwomen.org.uk/about-us/herstory/our-campaigns-2/ on 29/05/18

43 Women's Suffrage and Beyond under 'The Women Suffrage Timeline' at http://womensuffrage.org/?page_id=69 on 21/09/18

44 *Independent*, under 'Germany passes strict "no means no" rape laws in response to Cologne attacks' at http://www.independent.co.uk/news/world/europe/rape-law-germany-reichstag-mps-vote-strict-no-means-no-rape-law-cologne-attacks-a7125101.html on 29/05/18

45 Africa on NBCNews, under 'Liberian becomes Africa's first female president', at http://www.nbcnews.com/id/10865705/ns/world_news-africa/t/liberian-becomes-africas-first-female-president/#.WqpA0IIuAWo on 29/05/18

46 *Guardian*, under 'Egypt bans female circumcision after death of 12-year-old girl' at https://www.theguardian.com/world/2007/jun/30/gender.humanrights on 29/05/18

47 United Nations Foundations, under 'Key Dates in International Women's History' at http://www.unfoundation.org/assets/pdf/key-dates-in-international-womens-history.pdf on 29/05/18

48 BBC News, Middle East, under 'Women in Saudi Arabia to vote and run in elections', at http://www.bbc.co.uk/news/world-us-canada-15052030 on 29/05/18

49 *Guardian*, 'Women, under "Enough is enough": the fight against everyday sexism' at https://www.theguardian.com/lifeandstyle/2014/mar/29/everyday-sexism-women-encounter-laura-bates on 29/05/18

50 Council of Europe, at 'Council of Europe Convention on preventing and combating violence against women and domestic violence', https://www.coe.int/fr/web/conventions/full-list/-/conventions/rms/090000168008482e on 29/05/18

51 Nobelprize.org, under 'Malala Yousafzai – Facts', at https://www.nobelprize.org/nobel_prizes/peace/laureates/2014/yousafzai-facts.html on 29/05/18

52 *Guardian*, under 'The Gambia bans female genital mutilation' at https://www.theguardian.com/society/2015/nov/24/thegambia-bans-female-genital-mutilation on 29/09/18

53 *Guardian*, under, 'Page 3: The *Sun* calls time on topless models

after 44 years', at https://www.theguardian.com/media/2015/
jan/19/has-the-sun-axed-page-3-topless-pictures on 29/05/18

54 BBC News, Middle East, under 'Saudi Arabia driving ban
on women to be lifted' at http://www.bbc.co.uk/news/world-
middle-east-41408195 on 29/05/18

55 *Metro*, under 'Women who started #MeToo movement has
been helping sex assault survivors for 10 years', at http://
metro.co.uk/2017/10/17/woman-who-started-metoo-
movement-has-been-helping-sex-assault-survivors-for-10-
years-7005580/ on 29/05/18

56 Merriam-Webster, under 'Merriam-Webster's 2017 Words of
the Year', at   https://www.merriam-webster.com/words-at-
play/word-of-the-year-2017-feminism on 29/05/18

Further Resources

If if something has come up for you while reading this, here are a few resources that might help you to get some support or direct you to further knowledge about a particular issue.

Brook
Brook is an organisation giving sex and relationship advice to the under-twenty-fives. Their website is brilliant, and you don't have to be young to go on there. There is lots of information and further resources, so it could be a good starting place if you are affected by a particular issue, such as FGM, or if you need advice about contraception, gender identity, relationships or abuse and violence.

In addition to this, if you are under twenty-five and in the UK, Brook offers free and confidential appointments across the country.

https://www.brook.org.uk/

Scarleteen
Again a website for young people, but it is brilliant for the not so young too. It's really informative and doesn't assume you know everything and what every term means. I love it. So many questions are answered in a really upfront and non-shaming way. A quick look at the advice section at the time of writing shows questions such as 'how do I ask for lube?', 'I'd like to come out as pansexual but don't want to ruin my current relationship', 'Why

do rape scenes in TV shows give me panic attacks?', 'I'm not sure my girlfriend is enjoying herself during sex and I'm feeling insecure about it'.

http://www.scarleteen.com/

I loved learning and experimenting through workshops. But if you think you might want to do some workshops as I did, please do as much research as you can about teachers beforehand. Sadly, I had to remove some names from this manuscript, as allegations of abuses of power had emerged.

I do feel able to recommend these teachers I worked with, though.

- I learned about tantra with Roxana. Her website is www. thegreatintimacy.com
- I learned about conscious kink and practised the Wheel of Consent with Rupert. His website is www.artofconsent.co.uk
- I learned about intimacy with Jan Day. Her website is www. janday.com

Acknowledgements

Hold tight, beautiful people, these acknowledgements might well be longer than the book you've just read.

First of all, my heartfelt thanks go to everyone involved in this story. Thank you for allowing me to learn about myself in this way.

And secondly, thank you to everyone who pledged and made this book become a reality. It couldn't have happened without you. I hope, I really hope, you like it.

I was never really sure where this book 'fitted' in terms of the publishing industry. Early conversations with publishers made it pretty clear I was going to have to make some big compromises on content and title if it was to be published. But a watered-down book about female sexuality seemed a bit pointless to me. I always thought, 'If a publisher gets it, I will go with them.' Thank you Unbound for getting it. Thank you Peter Jukes for suggesting them and to John Mitchinson for being so lovely and buying me posh gin.

Everyone I have come into contact with at Unbound has been so warm and supportive. It's quite remarkable what you have created as a team and a company. It feels very special to be part of it. Big tas to Jimmy for helping me reach the target. And of course the wonderful editorial team. All along the way I've felt a bit small and terrified delivering each draft, thank you Anna Simpson and Imogen Denny all for your kindness and brilliance in overseeing it. To editor Justine Taylor, you were so gentle with me, I loved our time working on this. And Miranda, thank you so much for your thoroughness, and particularly your care for the rhythm of the book. I loved your suggestions. And also big thanks to Kate Quarry for a painstaking proofread which I fear exploded you; Mark Ecob for being so thoughtful and passionate in giving this such a strong cover; Amy Winchester for spreading the word in such a fun and warm way; and to Lauren Fulbright who produced such a beautiful book.

Big thanks to my agents, old and new, dear Rowan Lawton for early belief in this project and to Jo Unwin and Milly and the team for all your fabulousness and enthusiasm in it and me. I am very happy to be on board JULA.

Thanks to the kind people who have allowed me to share their words and work in this book, Annie Sprinkle and Beth Stephens, Betty Martin, Ruby May, DominantSoul, Kim Amani, the Summer House Weekend and Jan Day.

Thanks to the people who I tentatively first shared a chunk of the manuscript with, Michal and Rupert, for being so kind and constructive in your comments. Huge thanks to those valiant souls who ploughed through that first draft. I am so grateful to you Jo, Laura, Tamsin, Claire, Emily, Kathryn, Hollie, Anna Banana and Jane.

Massive thanks go to fellow 'flat-chested lezzers' and 'frigid bints', my No More Page 3 buddies for being hilarious, passionate and brilliant. You made the campaigning journey life-changing and life-enhancing. We did it! I so appreciate your being behind me writing this, you were quite within your rights to say, 'Don't do it, Luce, we'll only get more shit on social media!' But you didn't. I thank you.

I have been lucky to have had the support of a really wonderful group of women while I have been writing this book. Big thanks to my Red Tent sisters. I think I am able to be a little bit braver and bolder because of you.

Now then, a fair few years have now passed since I first sat there googling 'beautiful sex' that night, and without a shadow of a doubt they have been the most eventful and dramatic years of my life. Huge and heartfelt thanks go to those people who remained steadfast in their support and love throughout this time.

To my dad for, as ever, encouraging me and believing in me, even when the subject matter of what I was speaking out about was challenging for him. You are a truly amazing dad, friend and rock in my life. Thank you. And you, Mum, you are the wind beneath all our wings. I love you both so much.

To my dear Dan. Thank you for reminding me that I am always a frozen terrified mess at the end of every book, for bringing me food when I was campaigning and forgetting to eat, for all those little things you do and say, they all mean so much.

And finally, to Bell Tent Man. Wow. What a ride. Thank you for your gorgeous and ready smile, your healing hands, for all you have taught me and for allowing me to share as I have. It's not always easy, I know, But we are doing it. I love you, our family and our life so much. Thank you.

Unbound is the world's first crowdfunding publisher, established in 2011.

We believe that wonderful things can happen when you clear a path for people who share a passion. That's why we've built a platform that brings together readers and authors to crowdfund books they believe in – and give fresh ideas that don't fit the traditional mould the chance they deserve.

This book is in your hands because readers made it possible. Everyone who pledged their support is listed below. Join them by visiting unbound.com and supporting a book today.

Alana Bond
Nicky Bond
Susanna Bond
Sophie Boner
Debbie Brannon
Ruth Bray
Dominic Brewer
Lizz Bricknell
David Brimble
Ian & Caroline Brittain
Jody Broad
Sarah Brooke
Tristan Brooke
Lorayn Brown
Rebecca Brown
Lief Bruylant
Sophie Budden
Camille BugSi
Emily Bull
Bill Burdette
Mark Butcher
Imogen Butler-Cole
T C
Deborah Cannom
Iain Carey
Tara Carlisle
Nicola Cartlidge
Amanda Caswell
Andrew Catlin
Maggie Cavanagh
Helen Chapman
Jo Cheetham
Letty Clark
Charlotte Clarke
Lisa Clarke
Ian Clarkson
Evelyn Clegg
Henrietta Clemett
Julian Clyne

Carole Margaret Moore Cole
Rebecca Cole
Jane Colombo
Melusine Colwell
Philip Connor
Mauro Corso
Andrew Cotterill
John Coventry
LJ Cowan
Louisa Cowell
Katie Coxall
Lucinda Critchley
Kate Cross
Katy Cross
Graham Crowder
Lydia Crudge
Ruth Curtis
Tamsyn D'Arienzo
Rishi Dastidar
Trishna Datta
Nicky Davidson
Ann Davies
Sarah Davies
Kimberley Davis
Audra Daws-Knowles
Sue Day
Christophe de Aristizabal
Odile de Caires
Susan Deakin
Deborah Deasy
Tierra Delaney
Oliver Demaine
Heather Denny
Caroline Devlin
Jeanne DeWet
Grace Dhonnchú
Sarah Dilnot
Emma Dixon
Les Dodd

Laura Dodsworth
Tracey Donnelly
Shellie Dormand-Bean
Christine Doubleday
Jenny Doughty
Cressida Downing
Candice Dowson
Fergus Drennan
Mandy Driscoll
Tracy Duckett
Jane Duffus
Carrie Dunham-LaGree
Emma Dunkley
George Eckton
Lisa Edwards
Vanessa Eghardt
Jo Elliott
Sophie Ellis
Jane Elmor
Mark Eltringham
Nicola Elwin
Evie Embrechts
Charlotte Featherstone
Madeleine Fenner
Mark Fessey
Frank Filardo
Paul Fischer
Rowan Fookes
John Foord
Laura Forker
Penny Forsyth
Lynette Fough
Elena Foulkes
Clare Fox
Emma Franieczek
Isobel Frankish
D Franklin
Kirsty Fraser
Emily Freud

Eileen Fryer
Carole Garley
Melissa Gartside
Laura Garwood
Philippa Gaut
Ryan Gibberd
Elly Goodman
Patrick Gordon
Emily Gray
Mark Greene
Siobhán Grennan
Jacquelyn Guderley
Niva Gunasegaran
James Gwilliam
Paul Hamann
Harriet Hanmer
Alexandra Hannum
Sarah Haque
Amy Harbison
Steve Harcourt
Kate Hardie
Claire R E Harris
Jo Harrison
Victoria Haslam
Fay Hasnip
Abbie Headon
Henrietta Heald
David Heath
Jude Henderson
Tamsin Hewett
Catherine Higgins
Yannick Hill
Catriona Hillerton
Dana Hirsch
Titus Hjelm
Stuart Hobday
Marcelle Hogg
Grant Holmes
Mike Holmes

Katie Hughes
Kelly Hurst
Julie Hurst Hand
Gav In
J.S.M
Emily Jacob
Bonnie James
Martha Jay
Caitlin Jenkins
Lyndsey Jenkins
Britta Jensen
Brenna Jessie
Alex Jones
Charlotte Jones
Claire Jones
Dylan Jones
Emily Jones
Holly Jones
Marianne Jones
Tim Jones
Luna Joy
Peter Jukes
Michal Kahn
Aaron Kavanagh
Deborah Kearne
Kate Kearns
Scarlett Keay
Rachael Kerr
Dan Kieran
Katie Knight
Samantha Knight
Ruth Knowles
Sophie Kuhn
Julia Lally
Sean Lally
Georgie Laming
Briony Langley-Miles
Barbara Lapthorn
Steph Larcombe

Laura
Rowan Lawton
Jimmy Leach
Calu Lema
Hannah Lewis
Melissa Li
Sian Life
Claire Linacre
Hanna Lingman
Dan Lipscombe
Kimberly Logan
Mary Amethyst Lomax
Chris Lord
Isabel Losada
Carrie Love
Love
Karen Lowe-McAlley
Gina Luck
Adrian Lynham
Anne Lyon
Christine Lyon
Sheridan MacDonald
Honor Mackley-Ward
Cait MacPhee
Milcah Marcelo
Joe Marriott
MartinMcD
Emily Matthews
Julie Matthews
Tim May
Tom Mayer
Lisa Mccourt
Steven McKinnon
Jess Medling
Kat Metcalf
Julia Midwinter
Elaine Milligan
Rebecca Misch
John Mitchinson

Alex Mizzi
Grace Money
Bethan Moore
Neil Morbey
David Moreno-Dominguez
Charlie Morley
Neil Morrison
Sally Morrison-Griffiths
Chris Mousley Jones
Oliver Muller
Mike Murphy
Sophie Murray
Victoria Murray-Browne
Amie Mustill
Norah Myers
Carlo Navato
Serena Nazareth
Yas Necati
Prue Nichols
Katie Nicoll
Sakthi Norton
Lydia Nowak
Patrick O Connor
Tania O'Donnell
Julian O'Donovan
Kit O'Keeffe
Greg O'Toole
Lucy Oates
Christina Pacitto
Roxana Padmini
Anne Paine
Laurence Parkes
Nick Parsons
Sarah Patmore
Tash Payne
Lucy Pepper
Katherine Perfect
Charlotte Perkins
Anthony Pletts

Ulrich Pohanka
Nicola Pointer
Justin Pollard
Lauren Pollitt
Christine Pollock
Tony Poole
Anna Portch
Helen Potter
Kellie Powell
Jennifer Preston
Tara Pritchard
David Puckridge
R OB
Gwen Rahardja
Rainy101
Bea Ramsay
Claire Ransom
Pointibird Rashbrook
Biff Raven-Hill
Karen Rawlins
Charlotte Reed
Tori Reed
Elle Reiki
Nicole Reilly
Suzie Rigoulet
Gail Roberts
Hannah Roberts
Wyn Roberts
Miriam Robinson
Anna Roderick
Judy Rolph
Tessa Russell
Claudia Rutherford
Anna Sansom
Sarah
Riccardo Sartori
Helen Saxby
Gina Scalise
Frances Scott

Lynsey Searle
Millie Seaward
Mark Seddon
Karin Seidler
Michael Shaeffer
Sarah Shatwell
Kate Shaw
Raz Shaw
William Shaw
Katie Shellard
Hannah Sheppard
Jeff Sheppard
Emily Shipp
John Shirlaw
MD Sias
Emily Silva
Melanie Sinclair
Jenny Skivens
Eleanor Small
Drew Smith
Lesley Smith
Natalie Smith
Sam Smith
Julia Spaan
Serena Spencer-Jones
Martin Spencer-Whitton
Marc Standaert
Helen Staniland
Geoff Stanton
Glynne Steele
Philip Stewart
Katie Stowell
Corin Stuart
Dave Sussman
Mike Sussman
Simon Paul Sutton
Katherine Sydney
Matthew Sylvester

Boglarka Szabo
Paul Tallentire
Rosa Targett
Holly Tarquini
Lewis Tearle
Sarah Thelwall
Juliet Thomas
Mike Thomas
Richard Thomas
Hermione Thompson
Clare Thomson
Emily Thomson
Kathryn Thomson
Penny Thomson
Hollie Thomson (beautiful niece)
Jen Tidman
Gina Tomkins
Biba Tomulic-Leach
Angela Towers
Jamie Troy
Roberto Tyley
Lisa Type
Portia Ungley
Natalie Van Veggel
Nicola Vanderwert
Robin Vanner
Craig Vaughton
Veep
Paul Vela
L Vinter
Carolin Voigt
Natalie Wall
Rosie Walsh
Vicki Watson
Karl Webster
Kelly Webster
Tom Webster
Janice Welsh

Eldon Wethered
Alison Wevling
Emily Wheeler
Abigail Whitbread
Alan White
Hannah White
Liz Wilks
Tracy Louise Williams
Johanna Wilson

Kathryn Wood
Jessica Woodfall
Jane C Woods
Pippa Wright
Karen Wyrill
Danielle Young
Eben Young
Jane Zohoungbogbo